Cambridge English Readers

Level 6

Series editor: Philip Prowse

Solo Saxophone

Jeremy Harmer

T0094897

CAMBRIDGE
UNIVERSITY PRESS

University Printing House, Cambridge CB2 8BS, United Kingdom

One Liberty Plaza, 20th Floor, New York, NY 10006, USA

477 Williamstown Road, Port Melbourne, VIC 3207, Australia

314–321, 3rd Floor, Plot 3, Splendor Forum, Jasola District Centre,
New Delhi – 110025, India

79 Anson Road, #06–04/06, Singapore 079906

Cambridge University Press is part of the University of Cambridge.

It furthers the University's mission by disseminating knowledge in the pursuit of
education, learning and research at the highest international levels of excellence.

www.cambridge.org
Information on this title: www.cambridge.org/9780521182959

© Cambridge University Press 2011

First published 2011

Jeremy Harmer has asserted his right to be identified as the Author of the Work in
accordance with the Copyright, Designs and Patents Act 1988.

Printed in Great Britain by Ashford Colour Press Ltd.

Typeset by Aptara Inc.
Map artwork by Malcolm Barnes
Cover images: Alamy / © Roger Hutchings, © Getty Images / Jupiterimage

A catalogue record for this publication is available from the British Library

ISBN 978-0-521-18295-9 paperback

Contents

Characters

Katy Sullivan: a young reporter for *The Daily Witness*
  newspaper
Paul Sorensen: Katy's boyfriend
Caryl Jones: editor of *The Daily Witness*
Benjamin Cohen: a colleague of Katy's at *The Daily Witness*
Ed Jonas: an older reporter for *The Daily Witness*
Haris Osmanović: a driver
Colin Northcott: a TV cameraman
Carla Bosisio: a reporter for an Italian TV station
Željko Kojić: a saxophonist
Alberto Ricci: a TV cameraman
Borisav Popović: an army captain
Dragomir Milošević: an army general
Jack Hickton: an American mercenary

A song
Played on a solo saxophone
A crazy sound
A lonely sound
A cry that tells us
Love goes on and on

Alain Boublil and Richard Maltby, *Miss Saigon*

Author's note

In the early 1990s there were disagreements between the different People's Republics of what was then the Socialist Federal Republic of Yugoslavia. Croatia and Slovenia (two of the People's Republics) declared their independence in 1991. Fierce fighting broke out between Croatia and Serbia, another of the People's Republics. The ethnic Serbs, both in Serbia, and also in the Republic of Bosnia and Herzgovina, began a war of conquest or self-defence, depending on your point of view. Much of the fighting took place in Bosnia and Herzegovina, and in particular, its capital city, Sarajevo. For four years (from 1992 to 1996) Sarajevo was 'under siege' – it was difficult for people to leave or enter the city because of the soldiers who surrounded it. The Sarajevo siege is the longest in modern history.

Dragomir Milošević, a character in this story, is based on a real person who did, indeed, command the forces on Mount Trebović above Sarajevo. Everyone else who appears in *Solo Saxophone* has been made up by the author, and is not based on any person living or dead. However, it is true that music was used by many people to express their feelings about what was happening (including Vedran Smailović, the extraordinary 'Cellist of Sarajevo').

Yugoslavia in 1990

Overture *Children*

The moment she walks into the hotel room with the handsome soldier, Katy realises that she has made a terrible mistake. For one thing, he has changed and she doesn't trust him any more, and for another she doesn't know what he's going to do.

She's out of breath. They have walked up the stairs to the fifteenth floor because the lifts don't work. Nothing works in Sarajevo these days. There's no glass in the window, there are no curtains, and there's no bed. The room is a mess. But from the glassless window you can look down into the street below with its smashed cars and dirty dust-filled holes.

The soldier goes over to the window.

'Look!' he says. 'Look at them!' Two children, girls – aged about nine or ten – are running along a track next to the railway carrying something between them. It looks like a plastic can. It probably contains water. From up here they look very small, very defenceless.

'Which one do you want me to shoot?' he asks.

'What? What did you say?' Katy says in disbelief.

'Which one do you want me to shoot?' the soldier repeats.

'Don't be stupid.' She hasn't expected this.

'Come on! Hurry up. They'll be gone soon,' he says impatiently.

'You're not serious!' Katy's heart is suddenly racing. He's joking. He must be joking. Perhaps he isn't joking. Something terrible is about to happen.

He turns to her. He's smiling with that big wide mouth. His large blue eyes are shining in the late afternoon light. But now they are cold, dangerous, crazy.

'Children are more fun,' he says. 'They're more difficult to hit, because they're smaller, you see. It's better when you get children.'

'No,' she protests, 'no, don't say that. You can't mean that.'

'What am I involved in here?' she's thinking. 'This shouldn't be happening. It can't be true.'

'Come on! Before it's too late. You choose!' he shouts at her.

'Stop it!' she cries. 'You're mad. You're completely mad!' She goes over to him. She has to stop him. She has to.

Two shots in the silence. Two loud explosions in the hotel bedroom.

Oh, no. NO!

She can't look through the glassless window. She doesn't want to look. But she has to. This is what she sees: two little bodies lying in the dusty road, their plastic can leaking water into the dry earth. One of them moves an arm, she thinks. She stares and stares. She feels as if her heart has stopped. She's trying to understand. He raises his rifle again. Pulls the trigger. Another explosion. It hurts her ears. He seems satisfied. Now there's no more movement by the railway track.

She tries to speak. She opens her mouth. But there are no words.

He puts down his gun and turns to face her. She's pale, shivering, her eyes wide with disbelief.

'Your fault.' He laughs.

'What? What?' Katy says.

'That was your fault,' he says again.

'What? How? What are you talking about?' She's whispering.

'You didn't choose. If you'd chosen one, I'd only have shot one. But you didn't. So one of them is your fault.' He turns back to the window and reaches into his pocket for a cigarette.

Katy stands there. She doesn't know what to do. In the distance she hears a machine gun. An explosion. Screams. And then, softly on the wind, the sound of music, the sound of notes in the distance, the sound of a saxophone, high, sad and lonely, as if someone was singing a goodbye song for the two little bodies in the dirt.

The wind changes. The music disappears. She looks back at the man. He's laughing at her. She feels sick. She wants to hit him. To kill him. To turn back time. Anything. But she can do nothing.

She runs from the room crying, the tears pouring down her face, her heart breaking. The sound of each step down the many, many stairs is like the crack of a rifle shot, the death of a child.

'Oh, God,' she cries, her breath coming in great long gasps. 'What am I doing here? How did I ever get into this?'

Chapter 1 *The precise moment*

London, June 22nd, 1995. At first, it was a day like any other. Katy got up, showered, had breakfast with Paul, listened to the news. Then she got her things, kissed Paul goodbye and left the house. She walked down the road to the Underground station. She got on the train and travelled to London Bridge. Then she walked from there to the building where she worked – the offices of *The Daily Witness* newspaper.

For the first three hours after she arrived she sat in front of her computer, phoning her contacts and typing out what they told her. As usual, Katy was writing for the newspaper's younger readers. That was her job: she wrote 'youth-focused' features.

Her phone rang. And that's when Katy's life started to change. At that precise moment.

Katy picked the receiver up. The editor wanted to see her. Now. Katy made a face at Benjamin – her best friend at work, who sat at the next desk – and got up.

'Where are you off to?' he asked. 'What's the matter?'

'Jones,' Katy said. 'She wants to see me.'

'Oh, dear! Have you done something wrong?' asked Benjamin.

'I don't think so,' she replied. But she was suddenly nervous. Caryl Jones, the editor of the newspaper, could be very nice if she thought you were doing a good job, but she shouted at people when things weren't going well, and nobody liked that.

Katy knocked on the editor's door. 'Come in,' a voice said sharply. She turned the handle. Her throat was dry. She noticed that her hand was shaking slightly. She opened the door.

When Katy entered the room Caryl Jones was just getting up from behind her desk. She was a small slim woman of about fifty years old. She had short hair and designer glasses.

'Ah, hello, Katy,' the editor said. 'Come in and sit down.' She walked over and took Katy by the arm, leading her towards a large black sofa. She sat down and Katy sat down next to her, feeling uncomfortable.

The phone rang. Caryl Jones jumped up and went to the door. Opening it she called out, 'I said no calls. No calls at all. You know what that means? It means NO calls!' Her voice had a surprising strength for someone of her size. She closed the door sharply and came back to the sofa. The phone stopped ringing.

Katy was looking round the walls. On the few occasions she'd been in the room, she'd always enjoyed the photos of Caryl Jones with the Queen, Caryl Jones with the prime minister, and a more recent one of her standing between the actors Tom Hanks and Morgan Freeman at the Oscars ceremony in Hollywood before they knew which of them had got the prize.

'Do you like your job on *The Daily Witness*, Katy?' the editor asked. It wasn't the question Katy had been expecting.

'Well, yes,' Katy replied nervously.

'Good. I'm glad. I like your work.'

'You do?' Katy asked.

'Yes, of course. I hired you to attract younger readers and

you seem to be doing just that. Our market research shows that our fastest growth in readers is among the sixteen to twenty-five age group. And some of that – not all of it, but a lot of it – is due to the writing you've been doing. I particularly liked your piece on the digital future and what it's going to mean for the way in which people will communicate with each other – this "World Wide Web" we're learning to live with.'

'Thanks. Thanks very much,' Katy said. 'I think—'

'Yes, well we can worry about all that another day,' the editor interrupted, coming back to the present. 'I've asked you to come and see me for a different reason. I don't have much time, so I'll come straight to the point. I've got a suggestion. One that will involve big changes for you. But I think you're ready for them. Would you like to hear about it?'

* * *

After Katy had left Caryl Jones' office, the one thing she needed was to talk to Paul. Caryl Jones had suggested it. 'I know this is a big decision,' she'd said, 'so why not take a day to think about it? You can go home now and talk to your boyfriend if you want. But I'll need to know your answer by five o'clock tomorrow, all right?'

Forty-five minutes later Katy let herself into the little house that she shared with Paul. She was about to call out his name, but something stopped her. She went into the kitchen. The house seemed very quiet. But it didn't feel empty.

There were two wine glasses on the kitchen table. Katy stared at them. There was something wrong with that. She stood there looking at them. She knew that they 'meant' something, but she couldn't think what it was. Her brain seemed to have stopped working. But in the end she walked out of the kitchen, back down the passage, until she came to the stairs.

Katy removed her shoes. She climbed the stairs one by one. All the time the silence in the house was getting louder and louder. At the top of the stairs she paused, her heart beating wildly. 'I must be brave,' she told herself and walked towards the bedroom.

The first thing she saw was Paul's T-shirt on the floor by the door. Next a pair of women's shoes, black with heels. As she came round the door she saw a pair of jeans, untidy on the floor, a skirt, boxer shorts, underwear … clothes. Clothes everywhere telling the story from beginning to end. She raised her eyes.

They were asleep, exhausted, his beautiful body and a woman's – my God, the neighbour! She hadn't expected the neighbour. She stood there in shock looking down at them, studying the woman's blonde hair, her arm thrown over Paul's chest, the rise and fall of her breathing.

Paul's subconscious mind must have sensed that something in the atmosphere was different, even though he was sleeping. He opened his eyes just a little. Then he closed them again while his mind thought about what he'd seen. And then, suddenly, he was awake, pulling the sheet over him before sitting up, his mouth falling open in surprise.

'Katy! What are you doing here? You're supposed to be at work,' he said.

'I came home early,' Katy said quietly.

'Yeah. Look, I'm sorry. I didn't expect … This isn't … I mean …' Paul started.

The neighbour had woken up now, wide-eyed and afraid. 'Oh, Katy,' she said. 'I'm sorry. Honestly. This isn't what it looks like!'

'It looks like sex,' Katy snapped back, brutal.

'Katy …' Paul mumbled.

'What are you doing with *her*?' she shouted at him. Paul looked uncomfortable, ashamed. Katy marched over to the bed and pulled the sheet away. 'You!' she commanded, pointing at the neighbour, frightening herself and the other two by her unexpected anger. 'Get out of my house right now! Go on. Get out!' And then, before the woman could start dressing, Katy had stormed out, down the stairs, trying to stop herself from crying. She slammed the door loudly behind her as she marched out into the street. She went into the phone box on the corner and dialled a number.

'Hello,' said the voice in her ear.

'Mum. It's me, Katy,' she said, trying not to sound hysterical.

'What is it this time?' her mother said in her usual 'I told you so' voice.

'Can I come and stay for a few days?'

Chapter 2   *Benjamin*

As she travelled from her mother's house to the offices of *The Daily Witness* the next day, Katy tried to concentrate, but it wasn't easy. She'd been crying a lot and she'd hardly slept. It had taken a long time in front of the mirror when she'd got up to do something about her face. Her mind kept jumping from the scene in Caryl Jones' office to the horror of what she'd seen in her house – and back again. Her whole life seemed to hang in the balance. Doors opening. Doors closing. What was she going to do about Paul – if there *was* anything she could do? What was she going to do about her editor's suggestion?

Caryl Jones had asked Katy to go to Sarajevo. The suggestion had taken Katy's breath away at first and she'd said nothing. Sarajevo was a city under siege, in the middle of the chaos that had overtaken the country everyone used to know as Yugoslavia. Like anyone who watched the news, Katy had been horrified by the scenes of destruction and human suffering from Sarajevo that she'd seen on her television screen. 'That's quite a suggestion,' were the first words she'd said to her editor. 'But why Sarajevo? Why me?'

' "Why Sarajevo?" Well, because what's happening there is one of the most important stories of our time. We all know what's going on, but nobody's doing anything about it, even though it's a humanitarian disaster. It feels to me as if people are switching off – I mean in their minds as well as turning off their televisions. Someone actually said to me at a dinner party two days ago that he couldn't take any more of it. He said that the scenes on TV had stopped meaning anything any more. He was suffering from "war fatigue" he said. But that shouldn't be happening. And perhaps we in the newspaper business can stop it happening. I need someone who can write about what's happening in Sarajevo, so that our readers can experience it in a completely different way.'

'But *The Daily Witness* has got war reporters. Ed Jonas is there. He's much more experienced than me.'

'Perhaps. But Ed Jonas is coming home, so I need someone else to go out anyway. I've been thinking about who that should be. "Why me?" you asked. Well, I want more of our younger readers to take an interest. You just might be the person to make that happen. I don't want the usual articles, you see. I want something personal. I want someone to write about what it's really like to be there.'

So now, as she walked from the Underground station to the building where *The Daily Witness* had its offices, Katy had to decide what to do. If she said yes, it would be like running away, an instant reaction to having found her boyfriend in bed with another woman. But if she said no, she might be missing a great opportunity. But then again, did she really want to go into the middle of a war?

* * *

She sat at her computer and tried to think, but she found working impossible. Her mind was full of pictures: Paul and *that* woman, the images of Sarajevo that she'd seen on TV, Caryl Jones talking to her in her office. So when Benjamin came into work about an hour later he took one look at her and marched her to the lift, holding tightly onto her arm.

'What's the matter, Katy?' he asked a few minutes later. They were sitting at a table in *The Daily Witness* café on the roof of the building. From here you could see all over London.

'Do you really want to know?' Katy asked.

'Yes, of course I do,' Benjamin said.

So she told him everything – about Paul and about Caryl Jones's suggestion. He was silent for quite a long time.

'Well?' said Katy, when the silence had gone on for long enough. 'Aren't you going to say something?'

'Are you OK?' Benjamin said.

'Of course I'm not!' Katy replied. 'How would you feel if you found your boyfriend – well, your girlfriend, obviously …'

'OK, OK, sorry. That was a stupid question. It's just that …' he started.

'It's going to be awful at my mum's,' Katy said, trying to change the subject.

'Why? Don't you get on with her?' Benjamin asked. She'd liked Benjamin from her first day at *The Daily Witness*. He was the one person she could really talk to at work.

'Haven't I told you the story?' Katy asked.

'I'm not sure. You tell me lots of stories. I can't remember.' He was blond, about thirty-five and much taller than she was.

'We haven't really got on since my dad left when I was eight. It's not that she blamed me or anything. But she was so angry, so upset when he walked out that she just went crazy. She used to shout at me all the time. About nothing. At least that's what I remember from my childhood. She didn't give my brother a hard time in the same way. And we never got on after that. When I was a teenager it got even worse. I don't think I was much fun to be with, and neither was she. After I finished school I left home as fast as I could.'

'What does she think of Paul, of what's happened?' asked Benjamin.

'You can imagine. When I got to her house yesterday it only took her half an hour to say, "I told you what would happen!" And once she'd started there was no stopping her. "I knew he was no good. I told you never to trust a musician." My father was a musician, you see. "But you didn't listen to me, did you? You had to go and live with him without being married. Well, now look at you!" She had the time of her life telling me what a fool I'd been. She didn't even stop when I burst into tears. She's so prejudiced, so old-fashioned. Who cares whether Paul's a musician or the head of the Bank of England! He's a man, that's all.'

'Hey, wait a minute! We're not all the same,' her friend protested.

'Aren't you?' Katy teased him. Then, seeing his unhappy face, she said, 'Sorry. I'm just a bit tired.'

'Poor Katy,' said Benjamin.

'I'm not poor.' She was beginning to get annoyed. Ever since she'd left her house for the second time yesterday her mind had been racing, changing every minute from anger to despair, to excitement, and back to anger again.

'Sorry, Katy,' Benjamin said, 'I didn't mean …'

'Oh, it's OK. Really. It's just …' How could she tell him about the mixture of feelings running through her brain? In the end she just said, 'Thank you, Benjamin. You're a friend. A good friend.'

'I try to be. Right now I just want to know that you'll be OK,' he said.

'I'll survive.' She didn't want him to be too sympathetic. That would make her cry again.

'OK, OK. Let's change the subject. What are you going to do about Sarajevo? What are you going to say to our editor when you see her this afternoon? Are you going to go or not?'

'I don't know.' She was confused about Caryl Jones' offer. She was confused about everything right now, it seemed. If she went, what would happen with Paul? Could anything happen with Paul? If she didn't go …?

'Hello, Katy! I'm still here!' Benjamin joked, waving his hand in front of her face.

'What? Oh, sorry! I was miles away.'

'Yes, I know,' he said.

'Do you think if I went it would be like running away?'

'More like running towards if you ask me,' he replied. 'Straight into a war. I don't want anything to happen to you, Katy.' She knew he liked her, perhaps more than she wanted him to. She'd tried to stop it spoiling their relationship because she wanted to keep him as a friend.

'You think I should stay?' she asked.

'What I think doesn't matter. You have to make up your own mind,' was his immediate answer.

'Yes, I suppose I do,' she said.

Later on she went back to her computer screen, but she couldn't work. She kept thinking about Paul. Was it definitely the end of their relationship? Did she want to try and make it work again? How long had he been seeing the neighbour? Even if he was sorry, really sorry, would she ever trust him again? Questions, questions going round and round in her head. She wondered how long she could stand living at her mother's. She wondered what it would be like to have a father, a real father, someone she could ask for advice. She started to feel very sorry for herself.

Benjamin came over to her desk at ten minutes to five.

'Ten minutes to go!' he said. 'Do you know what you're going to do?'

'I've been thinking,' she answered.

'What about?' he asked.

'Lots of things. My life. That kind of thing.'

'And has it helped?'

'Yes,' she said. 'Yes, I think it has.'

'Well?' he asked.

'I'd better go. Caryl Jones will be waiting for me,' Katy said simply.

Chapter 3   *Don't get involved*

'Hello. Are you Katy?' a man said as she came out of the arrivals terminal at Belgrade airport. 'I'm Ed Jonas. Welcome to the mad world that used to be Yugoslavia. I think I saw you once when I was back in London.'

He was in his sixties. She remembered the day he'd come into the offices of *The Daily Witness*. They hadn't talked then, but she'd watched him chatting with her colleagues and laughing with Caryl Jones. A newsman through and through, that's what everyone said about him – one of the best.

When he offered to take her bags she refused to let him. She felt a lot stronger than he looked. They got into a taxi.

'Is this your first foreign job?' he asked. 'Your first war?'

'Yes,' Katy said.

'Well, I'm sure you'll be all right,' he replied, but he didn't sound sure at all.

Later they went to a restaurant in Skardalija Street, which Ed Jonas said was one of his favourites.

'Can I ask you a question?' she said after they'd ordered their food.

'Sure. Go ahead,' he said.

'Why are you leaving?'

'Why am I leaving? Well, this is my last night as a war reporter. I'm packing my bags for the last time. So I'll tell you, but no tears and sympathy, OK?' He poured her a glass of wine.

'I promise,' she said.

'OK. Well, I've got cancer, you see. I only just found out. It's not too advanced and it's possible that the doctors can get rid of it. But I'm not the healthiest person in the world, as you can see.'

'That's terrible,' Katy said.

'You promised!' he replied.

'Yes. I'm sorry. But why are you still smoking if you've got … if you're ill?'

'Funny word, isn't it, cancer? Nobody likes saying it. Why am I still smoking, you ask. Because I can't see a reason to stop. If I'm going to die I might as well die happy. Smoking is one of the few pleasures I have left. Anyway, back home they'll ban it one day, you see if they don't. I'll stop then.' He winked at her. 'Anyway I've got a wife and two grown-up children. None of them likes me very much at the moment. My wife says she wants to divorce me. But in a couple of months I'm going to be a grandfather for the first time. I think I need to make my peace with all of them. Now seems like a good time to go home in the circumstances.'

'Yes. Yes, I can see that,' said Katy.

'Hey, don't look so miserable. You're young and healthy, good-looking too. You've got some young man, I expect,' Jonas suggested.

'No, I don't think I have.' She told him about Paul and in return he told her about his life: wars in various parts of the world, the friendship of journalists, the cost to his personal life, the history of *The Daily Witness*.

They finished the bottle of wine. When the coffee arrived their conversation turned naturally to the situation in the country that had once been Yugoslavia.

'Sometimes what's happening here..., umm, what's happened here ...' He put two sugar lumps in his coffee and seemed uncertain about what to say next. 'Well, it just doesn't seem believable, does it? I mean, we're in what used to be called the Socialist Federal Republic of Yugoslavia. I know that it was always an impossible kind of federation. I know that. Six different republics, different religions, different races. But during the communist years, Tito somehow managed to keep it all together. And then when he died in 1980 it all began to fall apart. The Croats and Serbs in Croatia started arguing with each other, the Kosovans tried for independence, the Serbs got upset ...'

'And from what I know it all went really bad when Croatia and Slovenia declared independence in 1991,' Katy said, mostly to help him. He was trying to talk, but coughing at the same time.

'Yes,' he agreed, clearing his throat noisily, 'that's when the killing started. And the fighting has been terrible. Then, on top of that, when Bosnia and Herzogovina said it wanted to be independent too, many of the Bosnian Serbs weren't happy, and the Serbs from Serbia weren't happy either. That's when they started trying to "cleanse" Bosnia and Herzogovina of the Bosniaks – the Bosnian Muslims – and the Croats. They want to kick them out so they can have the place to themselves.'

'The thing I still don't understand,' Katy said, drinking her coffee, 'is why the Bosnians – the non-Serb Bosnians – don't fight back.'

'Well, they try to, but they haven't got the Serbs' weapons – tanks, guns, all that. They're fighting back as fiercely as they can in Sarajevo, but they're in a pretty bad state there.'

'The big debate back in the UK is whether other countries – I mean the USA, Europe – should do something about it. What's your view? What do you think the international community should do?' Katy asked him.

'The international community!' Jonas exclaimed with an angry kind of laugh. 'The international community says, "It's a pity of course, but we aren't going to sell arms to the people who want an independent multi-ethnic Bosnia and Herzegovina. We're not going to sell to the Muslims. It's not our war." It makes me so angry. When I think of Sarajevo, of how it used to be.' His voice faded. He seemed to be seeing the city he was talking about.

'Tell me,' Katy said. 'Tell me how it used to be.'

'It used to be the most amazing multi-ethnic city you could possibly imagine. Everybody – Serbs, Bosniaks, Croats, Montenegrins, Roma, Jews, everybody – used to live happily, side by side. But not any more. The Serbs are up in the mountains sending shells and bombs into the city, the streets are full of snipers and the place is falling apart. What is it that turns neighbours into killers? How do perfectly decent ordinary people get so crazy?'

'What's going to happen, do you think?' asked Katy.

'I honestly don't know. If the United Nations was a bit braver or if the Americans got involved, they could stop the killing tomorrow. But after Vietnam, Somalia, Rwanda – all those embarrassments – nobody wants to stick their neck out. Instead the United Nations sends a peacekeeping force like they always do. But haven't they learnt? You can't keep peace if peace doesn't exist in the first place.'

'So the Serbs will win? They'll get their Greater Serbia? Is that what you think is going to happen?' she continued.

'I don't know. The Bosnians – the multi-ethnic Bosnians – have fought the Serbs on the streets, and there are signs that the international community is getting very fed up. So it's, umm, just possible that they might do something sooner or later. But they'd better hurry up because most of the people who are trapped in Sarajevo will be killed unless someone comes and stops what's going on.' He started to cough again. He looked terrible. 'Do you mind if we go back now?'

As they got into the lift at their hotel, Ed Jonas gave her some advice.

'Out there in Sarajevo you have to be careful, all right? They don't usually kill journalists, but everybody makes mistakes. And Katy, there are snipers everywhere. Haris will do his best to protect you – he's the driver I always use in Sarajevo and he'll meet you when you get there – but there are other dangers too.' He suddenly looked more serious than at any other time during the evening. 'The most important thing, young Katy, is: don't get involved. OK? Don't get too close. If you stay objective, if you keep your distance, you'll be all right. If only I was thirty years younger!' The lift doors opened. 'This is my floor,' he said. He kissed her goodnight. She smelt the smoke and wine on his breath. He walked down the corridor without looking back.

* * *

'Why are you here?' the British soldier asked, looking at Katy in surprise.

'Because I'm a journalist, I suppose.' She wasn't going to be frightened. She hadn't even got to Sarajevo yet.

'Journalists!' he muttered. He was sitting opposite her in the army truck as it drove along the empty roads. It was painted white so that everyone would know it was part of the multinational peacekeeping force. There were three other soldiers with them, but two of them were asleep and the other one wasn't listening.

'Do you ever get attacked?' she asked the soldier.

'Yeah. Often.' Was he actually trying to frighten her? He was younger than her, all white skin and orange freckles. Under his helmet he had very short red hair. 'A friend of mine got shot in the arm last week. They sent him home. Lucky chap. This is the worst job I've ever had in the army.'

'Why?' she asked.

'Because we can all see what's going on, but we can't do anything about it,' he explained.

'Why not?' She was interested to see how he would explain their mission.

He looked really upset, as if he was going to cry. 'Because we're a peacekeeping force, that's why.'

'Well, isn't that a good thing?' she asked innocently.

'It should be. But all it means is that we're not allowed to do anything at all. We just stand around being nice to people, and any soldiers – it doesn't matter where they come from or what they think they're fighting for – can just walk right past us with big grins on their faces on their way to murder a few more innocent civilians and burn down their houses.'

'It's not that simple, surely?' she suggested.

'Yes, it is. Right now the Serb soldiers go from village to village, blowing up houses, farms, mosques, anything they feel like. They separate the men and the women – take them away, shoot them, or put them in prison camps and do all kinds of unspeakable things to them. They say they're "cleansing" the land of their enemies. "Ethnic cleansing" they call it. And the victims can't do anything about it because they haven't got anything to fight back with. And neither can we because our stupid government says we're not allowed to get involved. Oh, no!' he said suddenly. 'I forgot. You're a journalist.'

'It's all right. Don't worry.' Katy gave him her sweetest smile and watched him go red. 'Even if I write about your feelings I won't say who you are.'

They didn't talk after that. The truck roared on through the afternoon. It was raining as they passed through one empty village after another. Most of the houses had no windows or doors. In the beautiful countryside nothing moved.

Chapter 4   *From my hotel window*

They arrived at an army checkpoint on the edge of Sarajevo, where a group of soldiers was checking anyone who wanted to enter the city. She saw Haris standing behind the soldiers and recognised him immediately from Ed Jonas's description. He was a tall man and rather overweight. He waved at her.

Behind her the white army truck had turned round. She heard the engine roar as it left. It was going to the base of the peacekeeping force two kilometres outside the city.

A young man with a shaved head and a large gun checked her papers, looking her up and down as he pretended to compare her with the photograph on her press card. Finally he waved her through. She picked up her bag and the case with her laptop in it. She wished she hadn't packed so much, but when you're going to your first war zone you don't really know what to take.

'You are Katy,' Haris announced when she went up to him. 'I take your suitcase.' He lifted the bag from her hands. 'You come with me.' He walked off without saying anything more. Katy almost had to run to keep up with him.

'Hey, hold on,' she gasped.

'No. It is good we go fast,' he called back. She wasn't worried about his grammar, but his accent made it difficult for Katy to understand him. She'd have to get used to that. 'You are journalist, yes, but the soldiers, they are mad.'

They rounded a corner. The street was empty. There was a car with no wheels on her left. Haris pointed to an old Ford on her right. It was a dirty white. On the roof someone had painted 'Press' in untidy black letters.

'This is my car. You get in,' he told her.

Moments later they were bouncing along uneven avenues. Haris didn't just look ahead of him. He kept turning to the right and the left. She watched his eyes. He was looking into the buildings on either side of them. She wished he would keep his eyes on the road.

'What are you looking at?' she asked.

'I worry about snipers. These guys they sit here and shoot people,' he explained.

'What for?'

'Sport? Revenge? Crazy people? I do not know.' He shrugged his shoulders.

'Are we in danger?' she asked.

'Not too much. This is not their usual area and I have "Press" painted on the car,' he said proudly.

'Yes, I saw,' she said.

'I want us to be safe.' He smiled at her.

'That's good. I'm glad we're safe,' she said, but she didn't feel it.

'Maybe today it is different,' Haris offered, almost enthusiastically.

Not a very good beginning, Katy thought. She didn't know whether she was more worried about snipers shooting at her or about Haris's wild driving.

'How is my friend?' he suddenly asked.

'Sorry?' Katy said.

'Ed Jonas? How is he?'

'I don't think he's very well. He's a nice man,' she found herself saying.

'He is my friend. Perhaps I never see him again.' Haris lowered his head in sadness.

'I'm sure you will,' she comforted him, not sure if she believed it. A few minutes later she asked, 'Why are you in Sarajevo? Ed said that you're from Montenegro.'

'Sure. Yes. That is my home. But I came here for work four years ago and now,' he shrugged his shoulders and the car swung to the right, 'I stay. I do not know why. Perhaps I like the danger. Perhaps I am afraid to go home.'

'But I thought Montenegro was relatively safe. There isn't fighting there, surely,' she said.

'I have a wife,' he said unhappily, 'and many children.'

'Well, then you should go back to them,' Katy said.

'What do you know about it?' Haris sounded angry or upset. She couldn't tell which.

'Sorry, it's just that … well, isn't that what husbands and fathers do?' she asked.

'Yes. But I am here because there was not work in Montenegro and now …' His voice tailed off.

They drove on. The only other cars they saw were being driven as crazily as the car she was in. Everyone, Haris explained when she commented on it, was trying not to get shot.

Ten minutes later he pointed through the windscreen. 'There!' he said. 'That's your hotel. That's where all journalists are. You are all safe there because the Serbs do not shell it.'

* * *

After she'd checked in, Katy went to her room. It was very basic. There was a narrow bed with an old grey blanket. The chair and desk by the window reminded her of her old school. The mirror in the bedroom had a crack in it.

The bathroom was old-fashioned. She could see hard water stains on the showerhead and there was no shower curtain.

She unpacked her bag and put her clothes into two drawers beside the bed. She switched on the light and it worked. ('Not much electricity in Sarajevo,' Ed Jonas had told her. 'Nothing much works in the city any more. But your hotel has a petrol-powered generator. It's usually OK.' It looked as if he was right.) She plugged in her laptop and the battery charger for the satellite phone which Jonas had given her.

'What I want,' Caryl Jones had said at their last meeting in *The Daily Witness* offices, 'are articles telling us exactly what it's like over there. Remember what I said about our younger readership? The late teenagers, the twenty-somethings – they're the people who will read you. The older ones will too,' she added quickly when she saw the look on Katy's face, 'but I want something special from you which the older journalists don't give me. They think too much, they've "seen it all before". But you! I just want you, Katy Sullivan, to say what it's like for you to be in Sarajevo, what it's like to be in the middle of a war.'

'All right,' Katy thought. 'If that's what she wants, that's what I'll try and do.' She turned on her laptop and selected 'New Document'. But she couldn't think what to write. Perhaps she could talk about the history of the war? Or repeat some of Ed Jonas's views? No, that was no good. It wasn't what Caryl Jones wanted. She could talk about the soldier in the army vehicle. She could tell *The Daily Witness* readers what he said about the peacekeeping force. But that wasn't right either. It was someone else's opinion. Her editor wanted *her* voice, Katy Sullivan's voice, to be heard.

She looked out of the window beyond the desk trying to get some idea of how to start. She typed 'From my hotel window' onto the screen. 'That's it,' she thought to herself. 'I can tell them what I can see and what I think it means.' She began typing and now the words came easily:

FROM MY HOTEL WINDOW

From my hotel window, here in Sarajevo, I can see the hills and mountains which are all around this city. It's evening and the rain has stopped. The setting sun has turned the sky pink. The mountains look magical.

Although I haven't been here before I can understand why people say how beautiful this city used to be. It's not just those mountains – although being able to see them every day would make anyone feel good – it's the old buildings too, and the parks, and the Miljacka River. In Birmingham or Manchester concrete tower blocks look ugly, but here, because of where the city is, they could be almost attractive. Sarajevo should be a great place to visit.

But everything has changed from the days when people came here for pleasure. Now the hills and mountains are full of soldiers who want to kill people. The old buildings look as if they're falling down and even from here I can see bullet holes in the walls. The tower blocks have no glass in their windows. They probably have snipers waiting to shoot at you, my new friend Haris says.

Smoke is rising from a building on my left as I sit here at my computer. Down below me there's a park in ruins. The trees have no leaves. There is more mud than grass.

Everybody says that Sarajevo used to be a nice place to live, with Bosniaks (the Bosnian Muslims) and Serbs and Croats (and anyone else who was around) existing happily side by side for years. They ate in the same restaurants and went to the same cinemas. They watched the same plays and listened to the same concerts. They married each other, went to the same schools, and gave birthday parties for each other's children. Tourists used to come here. Then the war started and now everything is different.

And here I am. A war reporter in my first war. What will I find on these city streets? What's life in war-torn Sarajevo really like? What will happen to the people down there? What will happen to me?

I'll let you know.

When she'd finished she read through what she'd written. It looked all right. She saved it and wrote an email to go with it before getting out the satellite phone and plugging it in to the laptop. She dialled the number Caryl Jones had given her and waited while the connection was made. Thirty seconds later her email and her article had gone to *The Daily Witness*. She disconnected the phone and switched off the laptop. Time to change and get something to eat.

Chapter 5   *Colin*

The shower was much better than she'd expected. Katy stood there letting the hot water stream down her body and decided that she was feeling very positive. Despite the misery she'd felt as her personal life collapsed around her, she'd managed to make two big decisions. She'd told Paul that their relationship was definitely over, and she'd agreed to come here. She was doing what she wanted, acting only for herself. It gave her a delicious feeling of independence. Now she'd written her first piece as a war reporter.

All this showed, she told herself, that she wasn't just a person that things happened to. She was a person who made things happen. She turned her head up to the water and let it run over her face, smiling to herself. She began to hum a tune. For a second she couldn't think what it was and then she remembered. It was one of Paul's favourites, an old Bob Marley song, 'No Woman, No Cry'. Damn!

She turned off the shower, reached for a towel and dried herself. When she opened the bathroom door cold air from the open window hit her and made her shiver. Somewhere in the distance she heard the thump of an explosion, like a short burst of thunder. She remembered where she was.

She sat on the end of the small bed wondering what to wear. She was hungry. But eating meant going downstairs, and that meant meeting all the other journalists. What would they think of her, the new girl? Most of them had probably been reporting on this kind of situation for years.

Would they laugh at her? Would they be friendly or unkind?

She was getting quite cold now and the damp towel didn't help. She had to decide. In the end she put on a white shirt, a clean pair of jeans and her flat-heeled walking shoes. She put a dark-blue waistcoat over her shirt. She brushed her hair and put on lipstick and eyeliner. She studied herself in the cracked mirror. Her image came back slightly off-centre and unclear, but it was the image she thought was right. Casual but professional, smart and ready.

She took the most important things out of her bag and stuffed them into her waistcoat and jeans pockets. Then she turned off the lights and walked out of her room, closing the door behind her.

The dining room wasn't very full. Only four tables were occupied, each by a single diner. Two of them were reading books, she noticed, and another, who looked up as she passed, had a newspaper in his hand. She could feel his curious eyes follow her as she found a table near the back.

The waitress wore an off-white blouse and an old black skirt. She had tired eyes and it didn't look as if she'd washed her hair recently. When she came over to Katy's table she hardly looked at her, and took her order without interest.

The food, when it came, didn't taste of much. The soup was mostly water and the meat was too tough to eat. Katy ate three pieces of hard bread instead. When she'd finished she looked around her. A dead silence hung in the air. No-one else had come into the room. 'Anything is better than this,' she thought. 'I'll go and look for the bar. If there is one.'

There was, and it was full. Before she reached it she could hear the noise of conversation and smell the cigarette smoke. Now she really would have to face the crowds.

She stopped outside the open glass doors. For a minute she felt nervous and wondered whether she should just go back to her room. But she heard the voice of her mother – angry with her as usual – saying, 'What's the matter with you, Katy? Can't you face the truth of it?' And that decided her. Taking a deep breath she went in.

The conversation died as she entered and people looked in her direction. As she made her way towards the bar she knew they were all wondering who she was. There were only two or three other women in the room. She tried to look cool and unconcerned.

At the bar a man came straight up to her before she could order anything. 'Here, can I get you a drink?' he said. 'You look like you need one.'

She looked at him. He was thin and his cheeks were hollow. He had hard blue eyes and thinning hair. He'd been drinking for some time, she suspected. He was probably about forty.

'Yes. Thanks. That would be nice,' she said.

'Well?' he asked.

'Sorry?' She was trying to take everything in.

'What do you want to drink?' he asked.

'Can I have a beer? What's the best local beer?'

'Local beer? You're joking, of course! Have the imported stuff.' He was looking at her with a smile showing in the lines around his eyes.

'OK, thanks.' He was tired, she thought.

'You're from *The Daily Witness*, aren't you?' he asked.

'Yes. How did you know?'

'I heard the paper was sending out a woman reporter – a young woman reporter. There aren't too many of you here, you know. No, no, it wasn't that,' he joked. 'I'm a magician.'

Katy laughed. The ice had been broken.

'Is this your first war?' he asked.

'Is it that obvious?' She'd hoped to look more experienced.

'Well, yes, I guess it is a bit,' he replied.

'Everyone has to start somewhere, you know. Even you. You were like me once.' She picked up her beer.

'Umm, no, I was never really like you.' He was laughing.

'OK, OK,' she agreed, 'and yes, this is my "first war" as you put it. So what advice have you got for me?'

'Advice? Just go out there. Listen, look, watch. Write down what you see. Tell it how it is. That's the job.'

'You mean be objective?' she asked.

'No, I certainly *didn't* mean that.' He looked at her angrily.

'But I thought you said—' Katy started.

'Listen, look, watch. That's what I said. But I didn't say "be objective".' He was beginning to shout.

'OK,' she said to calm him down. 'I'm sorry.'

'Of all the wars I've been in,' he went on, as if she hadn't spoken, 'this is the one where it's not possible to "be objective". You can't be objective about what's going on here. Whatever they all say!' He waved his arm indicating the other people in the room.

'What newspaper do you work for?' she asked.

'I don't. I'm a cameraman,' he told her.

'So if you can't be objective, you must be a subjective cameraman.' She couldn't resist making a joke.

'Now you listen,' he said, looking her straight in the eye. 'You're new here. You're young. That's not your fault, but it is a handicap.' He was being very aggressive, Katy thought, but he was speaking with passionate sincerity too. She found it impossible to dislike him completely. 'Go out there and get some experience,' he went on. 'Talk to people. Find out how they live and die in this dreadful place. Then you can come back to me and we'll talk about being objective and you can make your jokes. Right now it's not worth my time.'

He got up and walked off. 'Thanks for the beer,' she called after him. He didn't turn back.

One of the other women in the room stood up and walked over to her. She was tall and thin with long black hair falling over her shoulders. She was wearing a striped jacket with a tie loosely knotted at her throat.

'Hi,' she said, in lightly accented English. 'I'm Carla.'

'Hello, I'm Katy.'

'From England?' the woman called Carla asked.

'Yes. You?' Katy said.

'I'm from Italy – from Channel 3 television.'

'Oh, right. How long have you been here?' Katy asked.

'A few months. Listen, don't worry about Colin.'

'Colin?' Katy asked.

'Yes. Colin Northcott,' Carla said, 'the man you were talking to. The best news cameraman in Sarajevo – the best in the business. Well, he used to be, anyway. I was watching you two talking. He looked like he was getting angry again.'

'Yes. I think I made him cross,' Katy said unhappily.

'No, you didn't. I mean, I'm sure it wasn't your fault. This war makes him cross, that's all. He's lost the professionalism that made him so good at his job. I'm worried about him.' Katy liked Carla's voice. It was warm and friendly.

'Yes, well he was pretty rude.' Katy laughed. 'He made me feel really small. I'm just sorry that I got him going.'

'Oh, don't take it personally,' Carla said. 'He's always upset these days. He's made the big mistake, you see.'

39

'What mistake?' Katy asked.

'He's become involved. That's not a good idea. This is not his war. It's not my war or your war. We just report what we see, but we stay outside it. We can't get too involved. We mustn't get too near.'

'That's more or less what Ed Jonas said,' Katy told her new friend.

'Dear old Ed. It's a pity he's gone home.'

'You don't "get too near"?' Katy asked, still thinking about what the Italian had said to her.

'Me? Of course not,' Carla said. 'I can't afford it. This is my job. This is how I make my living. Nothing more. Anyway, you want to come over and join us?'

Katy took her beer and went to sit with Carla and some of the other journalists. At first they all stared at her and one or two of them asked her questions. Then they got tired of being curious and settled back into the conversation they'd been having before Carla brought her over. They talked of narrow escapes they'd experienced, of arguments with editors and other journalists, of wives and girlfriends, husbands and young men. Katy listened, occasionally saying something, but mostly just trying to learn. Once she saw Colin the cameraman looking into the room again, a strange expression in his eyes. Then he turned and walked over to the hotel entrance and disappeared.

Chapter 6   *What war does to families*

When Katy came down to breakfast the next morning Carla was already sitting at one of the tables drinking coffee. She looked up as Katy walked in.

'Hi,' she called. 'Want to join me?'

'Sure. Thanks.' Carla looked perfect, her long black hair beautifully brushed, sunglasses pushed back on her head.

'So, how are you feeling this morning?' Carla asked her.

'Not too wonderful, actually.' They'd stayed up late last night drinking, as everybody's stories got more and more exaggerated and the laughter got louder and louder.

'No, me neither. Here, do you want some coffee?'

Breakfast was better than last night's supper. The coffee was dark and strong. There was bacon and toast.

'So what do you think of Sarajevo so far?'

'I don't know. I've hardly seen anything yet. But the view from my window is depressing – the parks in ruins, the tower blocks with no glass in the windows. I heard an explosion when I was upstairs yesterday evening.'

'Only one?' Carla asked with a smile.

'Yes. You probably think I'm stupid for mentioning it.'

'Not at all.' Carla put her hand on Katy's arm. 'But after a bit you get used to it.'

'Haris warned me about the snipers,' Katy said.

'Oh, you've met him, have you?'

'Yes. He collected me at the checkpoint.' Katy told her about Haris's wild driving.

41

'Well, he's right about the snipers,' Carla said after Katy had finished. 'They sit in those tall buildings, and when the grandfathers and mothers and brothers and children come out to get water they shoot them.'

'That's terrible,' Katy said.

'It may be terrible, Katy, but it's war,' was her new friend's reply.

'Sounds more like murder to me,' Katy said, shocked at what she'd just heard.

'War *is* murder,' Carla said.

'Don't say that in such a cheerful voice.' Katy was puzzled by the Italian's attitude.

'Oh, no. You mustn't misunderstand me,' Carla replied, as if she'd read Katy's mind. 'I'm not cheerful about all this. But there's nothing I can do about it. It's just the way it is.'

'The way it is?'

'Yes. War is murder. End of story.' Carla's cheerfulness seemed to have disappeared. 'At least we should be grateful that the Serbs don't come out of the hills and kill everyone in one great attack.'

'That's because of international opinion?' Katy wanted to hear what Carla thought.

'Yes, it's partly that. But they would face serious resistance here too. The Bosnians may not be strong enough to take the battle to the Serbs in the hills, but they'd resist a full attack to the last man – and woman. It's much easier for the Serbs to sit up there in the mountains and rain shells down. And the snipers are fairly safe if they're careful.'

'She's very sure of herself,' Katy thought, listening to the Italian. 'Good-looking, elegant, intelligent. I wish I was that sophisticated.'

'How long are you going to stay here?' Katy asked.

'As long as my husband lets me,' Carla replied.

'You're married?'

'Don't sound so surprised.'

'No, well it's just that …' Now Katy felt embarrassed. 'I'm sorry. You just don't look married, that's all.'

'How do married people look?'

'Oh, no! I've done it again, haven't I?' Katy bit her lip.

'Done what?' Carla asked.

'Well, last night I made that Northcott man cross and now I'm saying all the wrong things to you,' Katy explained.

'Look, Katy, I don't know you very well,' Carla said, 'but you know what I think? I think you should relax. And don't worry about me. I don't get upset easily. Anyway,' she laughed, 'I'm pleased. I'd be furious if I really did look married.'

'What does he do, your husband?'

'Oh, he's head of news at Channel 3 in Italy,' Carla said.

'Wow!'

'Yes,' Carla agreed. 'Wow! Everybody thinks I got my job because of him, but I was working at the company before he joined. I remember when he came for his interview. I didn't like him that much. He seemed too sure of himself. But when he started in the newsroom we got to know each other and I began to think he was all right. He must have thought I was all right too.'

'Doesn't he worry about you being here?' Katy asked.

'Yes. And I worry about him being there. In Rome. All by himself. That's not good for a handsome man like him. That's why I'm going back.'

'You're leaving Sarajevo?' Katy said.

'Yes. But not immediately. I'll be here for another few weeks. And after that …' She smiled.

'What?' Katy asked, noticing her expression. 'After that what?'

'Oh, you know,' Carla said, smiling. 'A family.'

'You're pregnant?' Katy asked.

'No, not yet. There hasn't been enough time. But we both want children. So maybe soon. Hey listen,' Carla said, changing the subject. 'I'm going out with Alberto, my cameraman, to do some interviews this morning. Do you want to come along? Haris is going to drive us.'

* * *

'Oh, no!' Haris roared as he saw them coming out of the hotel. 'The two most beautiful women in Sarajevo. Now they are together, I am lost!'

'You will be if you don't look after us properly,' Carla joked, walking over to the car without stopping. 'Come on,' she said to Katy. 'We'll sit in the back and let Alberto die of fright in the front.'

Alberto was a bit older than Carla. He was bald with round glasses and a grey moustache and beard. After saying 'Hello' to Katy and '*Buongiorno*' to Carla and Haris, he said almost nothing else for the rest of the journey.

Haris took them through narrow back streets until they got to the market. Here Carla interviewed three market traders, with Haris acting as an interpreter. The traders talked about how difficult it was to get food into the city. Some of their colleagues, they said, paid huge bribes to Serb soldiers to let food supplies through. Others just waited and waited, hoping that they would get supplies from the United Nations peacekeeping force.

'Don't you fear you will be attacked?' Carla asked one of them, a man of about sixty. When Haris translated the question the man got very angry and waved his arms around wildly.

'Yes,' Haris said to Carla. 'He is fearing attack all the time, all of the day. He says people is terrified, but they must to eat. He says before the war he had a neighbour, younger than he, a Serb who worked for him. Now same neighbour is a Serb soldier and he has to pay all his money for getting in food for his customers. He asks is this what his life is for?'

Later, while they were drinking coffee in a side street café near the market, Haris explained to Carla and Katy more about the lack of food in the city. Most people were going hungry, queuing for hours for bread and paying ridiculous prices for vegetables. But some people had started their own vegetable gardens, Haris told them, in places where the snipers couldn't reach them. And some supplies came through the network of Bosnians and those Serbs (and there were many) who objected to what was being done by their countrymen. They used underground tunnels connecting Sarajevo to the outside world.

Katy understood more about food and hunger that afternoon when they went to interview a woman who'd been a teacher at Sarajevo University. She must have once been pretty, but now there were lines of worry across her face and despair in her eyes. Her flat was in a neighbourhood that probably used to be pleasant, with children playing in the streets. But the streets were deserted now, full of burnt cars and holes.

The teacher's flat was a mess, with children's clothes all over the floor and the furniture. There were unwashed plates in the kitchen. One of her four children cried all the time

45

they were there. Another, a little boy, had a dirty bandage over one eye. There was no glass in the windows.

But when Carla talked to the woman, some sign of feeling came back into her eyes and she sat up straighter, as if suddenly her old self had returned. Alberto switched on his camera and the camera light brightened the untidy sitting room. The former teacher explained how she and her children lived and how she tried to keep her family together. It was a life Katy couldn't even begin to imagine. The woman spoke good English. She'd studied it at university, she told them, and had taken a teacher's course in England just before the war started. She was just like lots of people that Katy knew back home. And yet, surrounded by the chaos in her flat, Katy could think of nothing to say after Carla's interview. She left the apartment feeling inadequate, as if somehow she'd failed.

* * *

Back in her hotel room that evening Katy got out her laptop again. It was getting dark outside. Twice she saw flashes from the hills and a few seconds later heard the thump as the shells landed somewhere in the city, far away from the hotel. She switched on the computer, but for a long time she sat there staring blankly out of the darkening window. She thought of the angry market trader. She thought about a mother trying to raise her children in the middle of war. Which should she write about? What was the best way to explain to ordinary people back home what was going on here? How could she interest them as they sat in their trains going to work or fell asleep in their armchairs as they read the paper? She got up, walked around the room, thinking. But when she sat down again she knew what to write.

FAMILIES

Today I went to visit Nataša, a mother with four young children. She has shoulder-length black hair, which is going grey. Her clothes seem old and creased, as if they haven't seen an iron for weeks, maybe years. She used to be an attractive woman, I think, and could still be if things were different. Once, I imagine, she was bright and cheerful, but now she speaks with a heart-breaking despair.

Nataša's eldest child is ten years old and has only one eye. A dirty bandage covers the place where the other eye used to be, but he lost it when a soldier shot him 'by mistake'. Nataša's youngest child, a pretty five-year-old girl, has a bad ear infection and cries continuously from the pain. She needs medicine – antibiotics. There are no antibiotics in Sarajevo.

Nataša's husband, a lawyer, was killed six months ago. He didn't have a pension. Nataša has already spent her savings. There's no money in the banks. The banks are closed.

Six months ago Nataša was an English teacher at Sarajevo University. It was an important job and she was happy. One of her happiest memories is of her time in England, on a language-teaching course in Cambridge.

These days Nataša sits in a flat with broken glass in the windows and no heating. There is hardly any water to wash the dishes and the clothes. She doesn't have much food and she gives most of it to her children. It's cold at night. Sometimes she thinks she can't go on. But she's a mother.

Nataša is a Bosnian Serb. Her husband Emir was a Croat. They lived together in peace. It wasn't much to ask, surely. But this is war and war is murder. And this is what war does to families.

Chapter 7   *An invitation*

When Katy got out of bed and drew back the curtains the next morning she found herself looking at steady rain. Against the heavy grey sky she could see flashes of gunfire and the occasional puff of smoke. But neither the rain nor the sounds of war could completely destroy her feeling of satisfaction.

As she was brushing her teeth, she thought of the two emails she'd received last night. They'd been waiting for her when she sent her article about Nataša and her family back to *The Daily Witness*. The first one was very short. It read:

Liked your article. That's the style to continue with. Hope you're beginning to feel 'at home'.
Caryl Jones

The second one was longer and made her smile.

It's lonely here without you. I haven't got anyone to talk to. I insist that while you're out there, in the middle of your exciting war, you spare a thought for those of us left behind as slaves to the unforgiving *Daily Witness* and our terrifying editor!

Your friend (?) boyfriend (?) ex-boyfriend (?) came in this morning. He wanted to know how to get in touch with you. I didn't give him your new email address or anything. But he left a letter for you and asked me to send it. Should I have given him your email? Do you want me to send on the letter?

Your best answers would be 'No' and 'No', and then you can agree to come back to me. I'd be much better for you than he is/was. (Joke)

Got to go now. My sister has invited me out. Says she wants me to meet someone 'interesting'! Ouch.

Think of me out there.

Benjamin.

Katy was smiling to herself as she took the lift down to breakfast. Her boss was pleased with her, and Benjamin – well, he was a good friend. Did she want to hear from Paul? Not very much. All that, her past life, seemed unimportant to her now, even though it was very recent. When she thought of Paul, or her home, or her mother they all seemed to be from way back in the past, somewhere far away. Here was important now – Sarajevo, Serbs, Bosnians, Carla, Haris, the people she'd met yesterday.

She walked into the dining room and the first person she saw was Colin Northcott, sitting at a table right next to the entrance. She suddenly remembered the one thing she wasn't very happy about. Although Carla had tried to persuade her that he was 'a nice guy, really', she felt embarrassed when she thought of his opinion of her. He looked up as he heard her come in and for a second their eyes met before she looked away. If she'd continued to look at him, she might have seen something like a smile cross his face, followed by a hint of regret. But she moved on and found herself a table as far away as she could.

She needn't have bothered. He came over to her as she was pouring her second cup of coffee. He seemed embarrassed.

'Good morning,' he said uncomfortably. 'I hope you're getting on all right.'

'Yes. Thank you.' After their last conversation she was going to make him do all the work.

'Good.' There was a pause while he stood there. Katy added sugar to her coffee and stirred it in. 'You spent the day with Carla yesterday,' Colin said.

'Yes,' Katy replied.

'She told me off. Gave me a piece of her mind, you might say,' he went on.

'Did she?' Katy asked.

'Yes.' Colin paused again. He cleared his throat. 'Look, I … I feel a bit stupid standing here. Do you mind if I sit down?'

'Suit yourself.' Katy knew she was being rude, but she couldn't resist it. It felt good.

'Thanks.' He called the waitress over and asked for more coffee. 'If you don't mind?' he said to Katy.

'No, why should I?' she answered.

'I can think of a number of reasons actually,' he said.

'I can think of a couple myself.' She couldn't help smiling. He was trying so hard. And he looked better in the morning light. There was a silence.

'You didn't come to the bar last night,' he started. 'I—'

'No,' she interrupted. 'I went up to my room. Had an early night. The last couple of days have been quite busy.'

'It's like that at first.' He didn't sound rude or angry now. He was clearly trying to be friendly. 'But you have to pace yourself. You really do,' he went on uncomfortably. 'I've been in this business a long time. Well, it seems like a long time, anyway. Sometimes it gets too much and I say the wrong things. Like I did to you the night before last. Carla says I did, anyway. She says I was quite rude to you. Do you think I was?'

Now it was Katy's turn to feel uncomfortable. She wasn't sure what to say or why Colin had come to talk to her. She decided on honesty. 'Yes,' she said, 'I think you were.'

'You know,' he said. 'I'd like to forget our last conversation if you don't mind. You write whatever you want to write—'

'Well, thanks. I'm glad I've got your permission,' Katy said.

'All right, I deserved that. But if I agree not to tell you how to do your job all the time, can we start again?' he asked.

'Of course, only …' She stopped because she wasn't quite sure what she wanted, but she knew she wanted something.

'Only what?' he asked.

'Only …' Yes, now she had it. 'Only you have to agree to give me advice if and when I need it,' she said.

'Of course.' He looked relieved. 'Now look,' he went on, 'by way of apology, do you like music?'

'Depends what kind,' she said.

'That's a bit difficult to say. Umm, jazz? Rock? A bit of classical? That kind of thing?'

'Sure. I mean that's about all the music there is!' She was enjoying herself again.

'OK then,' Colin said. 'Why don't you come along with us tonight and we'll show you a very different side of Sarajevo and the people who live here? It'll cheer you up.'

'Who's "us"?' she asked.

'Me and Carla. We're just good friends,' he added, seeing the look on Katy's face.

'All right,' she said, getting up from the table. 'All right. Thank you, I will.'

Chapter 8 *Željko*

'The thing about this city,' Colin said from the back of the car, 'is that you really have to know where you're going.'

'That's original, Colin,' Carla turned round to say. 'I suppose that's what makes it different from other cities.'

'All right, all right,' Colin said, 'but you know what I mean. After all, this isn't like New York or Paris, is it? *You* understand what I mean, don't you, Katy?'

'Come on!' Katy objected. 'You can't expect me to take sides. This is only my third day here. I've only just met you!'

'Quite right, Katy,' Carla said. 'This is a private war between Colin and me.'

'I think you are crazy both,' Haris said from the driver's seat. They all laughed at that, though their laughter was uncomfortable and nervous.

Suddenly they heard the sound of gunfire to their right. In front of them sparks showed where bullets were hitting the road. Haris turned sharply and the car screamed into a side street.

Katy was thrown against Colin in the back seat as they bumped along the dark street. 'They were firing at us?' she asked stupidly.

'There doesn't seem to be anyone else on the road, so I guess they were. What do you think, Haris?' Colin was trying to sound calm, but his voice was shaking.

'I think that was too close. That is all I think.' He'd slowed down again. 'This is the second time this week I am nearly dead. Third time maybe I am not so lucky. Perhaps now I go back to my wife in Montenegro.'

'She must be missing you,' Katy said.

'Here you are. You have arrived,' the Montenegrin said, without his usual humour. He stopped the car. They were outside a café. Its lights were on, but there was no-one to be seen through the windows. 'Come on,' Haris said loudly. 'You get out now, quick.' Colin jumped out. Carla and Katy followed him. 'I come back in two hours,' Haris told them. 'You wait there.' He pointed to a street to the right of the café, where people were running inside through a side door.

'All right, Haris. Thanks. Be careful.' Colin's words were drowned as the car roared off into the night.

Carla, Colin and Katy joined the people hurrying through the side door into the café. They found themselves in a narrow corridor with a table at the end of it where two women were selling tickets. It was crowded. Katy didn't like being in small spaces and as if to make her feel worse, the lights went out. Somewhere in the building people groaned. In the corridor somebody laughed. Katy heard Colin say, 'Oh, no! Not again!' But he didn't sound worried, so she tried to tell herself that she wouldn't be either.

A light appeared at the end of the corridor where the table was, and then another and another as people lit the candles they were carrying. Carla turned round and, seeing Katy's worried face, tried to calm her. 'Don't panic!' She laughed. 'This happens all the time. Welcome to a nightclub, Sarajevo style. Come on, let's go down and hear the music.'

* * *

The stage was no more than a few boxes at the end of the basement room for the musicians to stand on. It was hot and crowded, and all the usual things like emergency exits and lighted bars were nowhere to be seen. When the three journalists walked in, a saxophone quartet was just finishing a tune. There was enthusiastic clapping from the audience, which made the candle flames dance.

'Come on,' Colin said. 'Let's see if we can find a table.'

They pushed their way to the front. There was one small table free in a dark corner by the edge of the 'stage' and they sat down at stools around it. Katy looked at the musicians. There was a woman in her early twenties with a huge instrument hanging heavily round her neck, curling away from her. Next to her a man with not much hair had a smaller saxophone. Another woman, well a girl really, played an instrument which was smaller than the man's, and finally, nearest Katy, a tall dark-haired man of about her own age was playing something which looked like a gold clarinet.

'That's Željko,' Carla said, following the direction of her eyes. 'Everybody likes Željko.'

'Everybody?' Katy asked.

'Yes. Everybody. In a way. Wait till you hear him play. Then you'll really like him.'

'What are all the different instruments?' Katy asked her. 'Do you know?'

'Sure. The biggest one, which Ajša's playing, is the baritone sax – it's like a cello, or the bass in a rock band. Then Josip, the man next to her, is playing the tenor sax. Selma, the younger woman, is playing the alto sax, and Željko, the handsome Željko, is playing the soprano sax.'

'He is rather good-looking, isn't he?' Katy said.

'Yes. Yes, he is,' Carla agreed. 'But with Željko it's more

54

than that. He's a bit of a nightmare really, when you get to know him, but he's also the greatest guy in the world. It's a bit difficult to explain.'

'You've got me really interested now!' Katy laughed.

'Well, don't be,' the Italian said. 'Not like that, anyway. Just enjoy the music. You will, I promise you.'

The quartet started to play again and it was immediately clear to Katy that they were very good. The music was – how would she describe it if she had to write about it? Dreamy. Warm. She suddenly found herself thinking of long hot summer afternoons, sitting on the bank of a river with the sun above her and a light wind in the trees. She had a strong, almost physical, memory of a day many years ago, with her mother and father. They were on a boat on a lake, in a park. Her father's hat was pushed back on his head as he rowed. She heard the sound of his laughter calling to her across the years.

The memory faded. She was back again in a kind of music club in the middle of Sarajevo under the eyes of a murderous army in the hills and soldiers in the streets. But when she looked at the other faces in the candlelight their expressions had changed too. The warm tunes and the soft sweet saxophones were wrapping them in comfort, taking the fear away.

The applause when they finished wasn't like the usual clapping in a theatre or a concert hall. It was loud, and people murmured or shouted their approval too. But what made it different was a strange feeling that the audience was grateful for the music itself, and this was mixed with a strong sense of community, a togetherness you could almost touch.

'What *was* that? It was beautiful,' Katy said.

'I don't know,' said Colin, 'but it was incredible.'

'I know what it was,' Carla said in a superior voice.

'All right then, what was it?' Colin asked.

'The third movement of the String Quartet by Debussy – arranged for saxophone quartet, of course.'

'How come you know about Debussy?' Colin asked.

'Why shouldn't I?'

'No, no reason. I was just surprised. That's all.'

'I seem to surprise everybody,' Carla replied, looking straight at Katy and laughing.

'Go on,' Katy responded to her glance. 'How come?'

'Oh, I studied music at university in Rome.'

'So you play an instrument?' Katy asked.

'Used to,' Carla said. 'The piano. I was never that good. And anyway, music wasn't exciting enough for me. It was useful though. I played piano in a bar while I studied journalism at night school. That was after university.'

'Do you still play?' Katy asked.

'No. What's the point?' Carla shrugged.

'But surely …' Katy started.

'These days I prefer to listen.'

'He makes a beautiful noise, the interesting-looking one,' Katy found herself saying dreamily. 'The tone of his instrument … It was out of this world. It was so …'

'Sexy?' Carla suggested.

'Yes.' Katy laughed. She'd been watching Željko. She liked the way he closed his eyes when he played, as if his instrument was doing all his talking, all his seeing, all his listening. She'd noticed his hands and the way his long thin fingers worked the keys of the saxophone. He was the kind of player that made you want to watch him as well as listen to him. His smile when people applauded had been absolutely genuine, as if he was really delighted.

'Well, you enjoy Željko. I'm just going over there to talk to Vlada and Imrana,' Carla said, and Katy watched as her friend got up and walked over to a couple standing by the door. The three of them began talking. When Katy turned back, Colin was smiling and Željko was coming over to their table.

'You are not from here,' the musician announced when he arrived, looking straight at her.

'No, I'm a journalist,' Katy said.

'Another journalist!' he said, unimpressed.

'I try to write about what I see,' she replied.

'All right. That is something, I suppose. Can I sit here?'

'Don't mind me,' Colin said, standing up. 'I'm going to get some drinks.'

'What about you?' Željko asked Katy, ignoring Colin. 'Will you give your permission for me to sit here?'

'Of course.' The musician sat on the stool Carla had been using. Someone brought a beer and gave it to him. 'Why are you a journalist?' he started.

'Stop right there,' she joked. 'I ask the questions.'

'OK, OK.' He put his hands up as if she was pointing a gun at him. 'I surrender.' Then, when he realised what he was doing, his smile disappeared and he put his arms down again, looking embarrassed.

'Where did you play before ... before all this?' she asked quickly.

'I was – that is, I still am, officially – a postgraduate student at the Royal Academy of Music in London.'

'So why are you here and not there?' she wondered.

'I came back when the war started. My father went to fight. I was worried for my mother, my sister,' Željko said.

'Are they all right?' Katy asked.

'My father was killed in the first week.'

'I'm sorry.' It was all she could think of to say.

'Everybody has lost somebody.' He said it as a matter of fact, nothing more or less.

'And your mother? Your sister?'

'They escaped. They left the city. They are in South America now.'

'So why don't you leave and join them,' she asked, puzzled, 'or go back to college in London? You could. You wouldn't have any trouble getting back into England. Or perhaps you can't leave?'

'No. I could leave,' he said. 'There are ways of leaving. But I do not want to go.'

'Why not? What about your studies?'

'Studies! I do not want to *study* music any more. I want to play it. Now. Here. In Sarajevo. Look around you. Look at this city, at Yugoslavia, at Bosnia and Herzogovina, at my country. The world is crazy. It is too important for studies.' He suddenly looked straight at her. He was so serious, so intense that she had to lower her eyes. 'No,' he said, touching her hand. 'Look at me. Look at me. I want you to understand.'

Slowly she raised her face again. His eyes were shining in the candle flame.

'This is how it is,' he went on. 'Here we all are suffering, we are dying. My father. My friends. Two of the violinists from the symphony orchestra who studied with me at university. My uncle, many more. We are a city of funerals,

58

a city of cemetries. So of course I want to go to South America or back to London. I am frightened. But I cannot.'

'Why not?' Katy asked.

'Because the streets of this city, my home, are covered in blood. It is the blood of my family, of my friends, of my countrymen. Their spirits are here. They tell me I cannot go. It is sacred ground. I have to stay to keep them company.'

'But what will happen if you too …?' She didn't finish her question.

'If it happens, it will happen. But before it does, I have music, something to give, something to remind myself, all of us, even visiting journalists, about life and love and beauty.'

'Music is that important?' Katy asked.

'Music is everything,' he said, his voice rising passionately. 'Language without words – straight into your heart. It does not even have to go into your brain first. You do not have to think. You just feel. Colour. Emotion. Everyone can understand it even if they do not know why. It can tell you how beautiful something is. Or it can make you angry. Sometimes it can make you laugh. And sometimes,' he said, his eyes looking into the distance, 'sometimes it can tell you that there is something better than just survival, something as good as friendship and sadness, something to make this terrible cruel world a thing to be in love with. Life. Life. Music is life.'

'I love your music,' she said, hardly daring to speak.

'I do not play so well.' He laughed.

'You play beautifully,' she protested.

'Thank you. I play for you as well.' He lifted his hand to her cheek. She felt the touch of his skin on her skin, soft and warm. It seemed to spread all over her body. She couldn't think of anything to say. Her heart seemed to stop and she felt a huge wild pulse of hope. She could hardly breathe.

'You will come again,' he announced.

'Yes, I will,' she promised.

'I will wait for you. Please come soon.' He got up. The other musicians were waiting for him on the little stage.

Colin came back with some beers. 'How did you get on with Željko?'

'He's …' Katy couldn't think of any words to describe her excitement. 'He's wonderful.'

'That's what all his girlfriends say!' Colin joked.

'I'm not a "girlfriend",' she started, but she saw the smile on his face and stopped, laughing herself.

'Just be careful though,' he said, suddenly becoming more serious. 'It's easy to admire Željko, love him even. At least that's what they say. Everyone does, apparently. But they don't get anything in return. He gives everything he has when he plays.'

'Well, thanks for the advice, Uncle Colin,' she said half angrily. She was going to say more, but Colin suddenly looked hurt and unhappy. Anyway, the quartet had begun to play again. This time they played an old Beatles number, a famous Whitney Houston song, and music by Oasis and Ocean Colour Scene. The four saxophones seemed to be chasing each other, the notes bouncing off the walls, making everybody in the darkened room smile. They made her smile too, made her feel like dancing. And for a moment in that cellar there was no war, no suffering and no death, just people. Music. A future.

Chapter 9   *Good guys, bad guys*

Katy went back to the basement to watch Željko play with his quartet more than once in the weeks that followed. Each time she saw him her heart seemed to stop. He was so passionate, so intense. The sight of his strong face and dancing fingers made her feel real and happy. It added to the excitement of the situation she was living and working in. She'd become used to the danger of life in Sarajevo, used to the sad stories from the people who lived here. Each day, she felt she was becoming more professional, a better reporter, like Carla, cool and effective. And the life she was leading was good, she had to admit, despite the terror all around her. She wrote her pieces for the paper, played with danger and sat in the hotel bar exchanging stories with the other journalists. In a few weeks she'd begun to feel as if she might even be their equal.

Željko wasn't nearly as interested in her as she was in him. True, he came over to speak to her when she went to see him play, but he only stayed for a minute or two each time, often shorter – she noted, than the time he spent with some of the other women there. There was no repeat of his magic touch or the direct intensity of his beautiful eyes.

Colin enjoyed joking about the musician with her. 'You're just another girlfriend to add to his collection,' he said. She told him, yet again, that she wasn't a girlfriend, or anything like it. But occasionally, when Colin joked, there was sadness in his eyes. He looked at her in the same way that Benjamin had sometimes done.

Now that they were friends – and they were friends, she realised with a smile – Colin no longer shouted at her and made her feel stupid even when he'd had too much to drink. He would still disagree with her, but there was no unpleasantness in his voice. He no longer treated her as a young reporter who knew nothing.

But it was probably Colin's arguing and her own curiosity about the 'other side' which made her agree with Carla's suggestion that they should go and interview some Serb soldiers. It wasn't, she told herself, a crazy idea. Journalists had a responsibility to inform and to explain – whoever they were writing about. It would be a good thing if she was able to tell her readers about some of the people who were turning Sarajevo into a living hell.

Not many journalists had gone up into the mountains that overlooked the city. Mostly this was because of fear. A cameraman and a news reporter had been killed three months ago because the soldiers had thought they were working for the enemy. Even when they'd shown their press passes, so the story went, the soldiers hadn't believed them and had shot them on the spot.

'But that was three months ago,' Carla protested when they were talking about it in the bar. 'A lot has changed since then. They've woken up to the fact that they don't have international support. We're just what they need.'

'That's exactly what I'm afraid of,' Katy said with feeling.

'Look,' her Italian friend said excitedly. 'It's going to be OK. I got my boss – all right, my husband – to get an Italian officer on the peacekeeping force to make contact with the Serb general up there, a guy called Milošević ... No, not the Serb leader,' she said when they all laughed.

'Just another guy with the same family name. And Haris says he'll drive us up there. So everything's all right. Alberto says he'll come, and you know what he's like.'

Katy did know what Carla's cameraman was like. He was silent. Serious. Professional. If he was prepared to go up into the hills, then she couldn't say no. Anyway, she told herself, Caryl Jones would approve. She'd loved some of Katy's earlier reports, but she'd told her by email that her last two or three reports had lacked the interest of the first few. Perhaps this was a chance to make things better.

'All right, I'll come. Yes, I'll definitely come,' she said, suddenly liking the idea. 'Only, don't tell Colin. He'll be furious.'

'Of course he won't,' Carla laughed. 'He likes you.'

* * *

But Colin *was* furious when he found out. Katy tried not to tell him, but it was impossible to lie to him.

'Are you going to hear the quartet tonight?' he asked her when they met at breakfast two days later.

'No, not tonight,' she said, trying to look innocent.

'Why not? They're moving out of the cellar.'

'What do you mean?'

'They're playing on the steps of the old concert hall, for a change,' Colin told her.

'Isn't that dangerous?'

'Well, sure, but everything's dangerous with the Serbs up on the hills. Your Željko—'

'He's not my Željko!' Katy protested.

'Your Željko says he's tired of playing in dark cellars,' Colin went on as if he hadn't heard her. 'Everyone in the quartet – and all the other musicians – are tired of playing in cellars.

It's time they took a stand, he says. So they're going to play in the place where they used to perform in their money-earning days before all this started.'

'He's amazing, isn't he?' she said, thinking of the handsome Bosnian.

'Whatever you say,' Colin replied. 'So are you going?'

'No. Not this evening. I can't,' she said guiltily. 'I've got something on this afternoon, you see. I don't know if I'll be back in time.'

'So it's true,' Colin said quietly.

'What? What's true?' She wanted him not to know.

'You're going up to Mount Trebović.' He was accusing her.

'Who told you?'

'That doesn't matter. Please don't do it.' He was almost begging her.

'Oh, come on, Colin, I'm a reporter,' Katy protested.

'Yes, but you're a human being too.'

'Of course I am. But it's my job, surely, to tell both sides of the story.'

'Both sides? Both sides! How many times do I have to tell you? There are the good guys and the bad guys. The good guys are down here with us. The bad guys ...' he pointed out towards the hills, 'the bad guys are up there. They've developed what they call modified air bombs, a mixture of shells and bombs – and they're designed to kill as many people as possible. Crowds of people. That's how bad they are. Don't you see? That's the story, that's the only story. You don't have to go up there to tell that story.'

'Well, I think I do.' She wasn't going to let him change her mind.

'The confidence of youth! No, I'm sorry,' he said quickly. 'I didn't mean that. But surely you must see how it is.'

'I understand that the people down here are in a terrible situation, yes.' She really wanted him to understand. 'I know there's fighting on the streets and it's not just one side that's doing it. I know there are Serbs up there in the hills and they're the ones who are shelling the city. But I want to know why. I want to tell my readers something about why – about what the people down here and up there are like.'

'Ha! My readers! How quickly you've changed. All right then, go. Go and talk to those murderers. If that's what makes you happy.'

'It doesn't make me happy, Colin. It's my job. I'm just trying to do my job, all right?' Now she was angry with him, angry that he was trying to make her feel bad. She got up and headed for the door.

'Katy,' he called after her as she went. 'Please be careful. The bad guys can be really bad – even to people like you.'

'Yeah,' she shouted back, 'but why should you care? Like you said, I've really changed.' And feeling pleased with herself for her sharp reply, she almost ran down the corridor towards the lift.

Chapter 10 *Roadblock*

Inside Haris's old Ford there was an air of tension as the Montenegrin drove rapidly through the afternoon streets. At one point they saw a middle-aged couple running along the pavement. As they passed the man fell, though whether he'd been shot was impossible to say.

'Shouldn't we …?' Katy started to ask. But she'd been in Sarajevo a few weeks now, and the question died on her lips. They sped past. As Katy looked back she saw the woman on her knees beside the fallen man. She would never find out who they were or what happened to them.

At a checkpoint outside the city Serb soldiers looked at their documents. They asked Haris some questions which Katy, Carla and Alberto couldn't understand. Haris's answers were softer than usual, more urgent.

But they were waved through after a few minutes and they headed in the direction of the hills. As soon as they'd driven round a corner, out of sight of the checkpoint, Carla laughed. 'Well done, Haris,' she said, slapping him on the back. 'I hope that wasn't too difficult.'

'Difficult! That was not difficult. Difficult is now,' he said, looking round at her. 'I wish I did not agree to this plan for you. I have bad feeling in my stomach.' He patted himself dramatically, all the time staring at Carla with troubled eyes.

They drove on in silence. To her surprise, and perhaps because of the previous night in the bar, Katy felt sleepy, and before she could do anything about it, her eyes were closed and she was asleep.

* * *

'Haris! Look out!' Alberto was shouting in panic from the front seat, before screaming something in Italian. Katy was suddenly wide awake. Alberto was reaching over to the steering wheel, trying to pull it towards him.

'What are you doing?' Haris shouted. But when he too saw the truck coming towards them he pulled at the steering wheel. Somehow, they just missed having an accident that would probably have killed them all.

'*Mamma mia!*' Alberto said and crossed himself. Katy felt sweat running down beneath her T-shirt.

'Hey, Haris,' Carla laughed nervously, 'please be careful. We don't want to be killed even before we get there.'

'I tell you,' he replied, clearly offended by the criticism of his passengers. 'It is going to be a bad day.'

They turned off the main road and started the climb upwards. For the next forty-five minutes the journey was uneventful. There was almost no traffic on the roads as they climbed out of the valley of Sarajevo. Once an army vehicle passed them, but it was green, not the white of the peacekeeping force. 'Serbs,' Alberto said, pointing at it. But the vehicle didn't stop or try to stop them.

They passed burnt-out cars and farm buildings and gradually, as they got higher and higher, stopped talking. Katy knew that the others were just as nervous as she was. She thought of the journalists that had been killed and started to wish that she hadn't agreed to this crazy scheme. But then she reminded herself that she was a journalist too, that this was what she was supposed to be doing and what

Caryl Jones would want her to do. Yes, she was nervous, but she was also excited by the thought of danger and of the story she was going to write.

They came round a corner and Haris put his foot on the brake. He swore. At least that's what it sounded like.

'This is it,' Alberto said quietly.

In front of them the road was blocked by two army trucks and about twenty soldiers carrying rifles, pistols, machine guns and knives. They were standing across the road, waiting.

Haris switched off the engine. They sat there, wondering what was going to happen. Katy felt her heart beating in her chest. She looked at the others and saw the worried looks on their faces. She realised that she was afraid.

Within two minutes the car was surrounded. One of the soldiers, a young man of about seventeen or eighteen, no more than a boy really, opened the driver's door and pulled Haris out of the car. As he did so he saw the women inside and whistled. He called to his friends. When they saw Katy and Carla they laughed. In no time at all they'd dragged the two reporters and Alberto from the car as well.

'Stay calm,' Carla said out of the corner of her mouth. Katy thought of telling her not to be silly, that she'd never felt less calm in her life, but she didn't. She was too scared to speak.

They stood in a line against the car, two men and two women. Katy looked across at Haris, but he refused to look back. He must have known that the slightest move, the slightest wrong look, might get them killed.

The soldiers stood back, their guns at the ready. Katy felt defenceless and rather foolish. She suddenly remembered Colin's disapproval and feared that he'd been right.

One of the soldiers pushed his gun into Haris's stomach and shouted at him in a threatening voice. Haris knelt down. He put his hands up and started to talk, fast, urgently. He looked in the direction of the journalists and talked even faster. He pointed at them, and the soldier hit him across the face.

'Stop that!' Katy said in a determined voice, which surprised her. 'Leave Haris alone. We're journalists. Press,' she explained, pointing to the card which hung from her neck. She hadn't meant to speak.

'Don't be silly,' Carla said quietly. 'Don't say anything.'

But Katy had started now, and she walked forward, pulling the press card from around her neck and holding it in front of her. 'We're press, journalists. We've come to report the Serb side of the war. Press!' she said again, desperately, as the boy soldier came towards her. Suddenly he pulled a pistol from his belt and held it against her head. She froze. This was it. He was going to shoot her. Now she was really, really frightened. Her legs were shaking. She didn't dare to turn her head. She tried to catch Carla's eye, but her Italian friend was looking away. The boy soldier was shouting in her ear, making ugly cruel sounds, words that she couldn't understand. His voice was getting louder and louder, higher and higher. 'Any second now,' she thought, 'any second now he's going to pull the trigger.' She could feel the pistol against her head.

Behind her she could hear Haris's voice, arguing, desperate. Now Carla was speaking, first in English and then in Italian. Katy heard the words 'press' and 'journalist' many times in both languages. Out of the corner of her eye she saw two soldiers drag Carla forward.

Time seemed to go very slowly then. She saw Carla slap one of the soldiers round the face and watched in horror as he used his rifle to punch her in the stomach in reply. Katy felt the boy soldier next to her, the one with the pistol, tense in anger. She thought she could feel his finger tighten on the trigger.

She was certain that now, this minute, she was going to die, and she was furious at the stupid senseless waste of her life. She was terrified that they were going to do something terrible to Carla too, and because she couldn't see behind her, she had no idea what was happening to Haris and Alberto. She closed her eyes.

She heard a machine gun firing and the noise of a vehicle. She waited for the pain, waited for the feeling of death. But nothing happened. Then the boy soldier gasped and moved away from her. The pistol was no longer pressing into the side of her head. She opened her eyes.

An army jeep had pulled up next to the line of soldiers. A man in uniform holding an AK-47 jumped out and walked towards them. All the soldiers had stopped laughing. They weren't looking at the journalists any more. This man was obviously the officer in command.

He shouted something at the soldiers standing next to Carla and Katy and within seconds the men had lowered their guns and run back to the others. As if in a dream Katy watched their faces. They looked unhappy, guilty, like schoolboys caught doing something wrong, she thought. Then, the moment the officer stopped talking, all the soldiers ran to the two trucks and climbed in. The two vehicles turned round and waited with their engines running, facing up the hill towards the Serb positions.

The officer came up to them and touched his cap with his right hand. He had dark weather-beaten skin, bright brown eyes and a thick moustache.

'I must apologise,' he said, looking from one to another of the frightened group. 'This was not the way to treat people like yourselves. You' – he looked from one to the other until he was looking directly at Carla – 'must be Mrs Bosisio. We have been expecting you. My General says hello and wishes to welcome you. My men ...' he pointed back to the two trucks, 'they are very young, very inexperienced.'

'Yes,' Carla exploded, 'and dangerous!'

'I am terribly sorry. It will not happen again,' said the officer in perfect English. 'The men will be punished. Allow me to introduce myself. I am Captain Borisav Popović. I have come to meet you and take you up to our positions.'

Katy looked at Carla and Alberto, and then at Haris, who was wiping the blood from his mouth where the soldier had hit him. She wondered if she looked as frightened as they did. 'Do we go on?' she asked. Alberto looked questioningly at Carla.

'Yes. I say we go with Capain Popović here,' Carla said to them all. She was obviously still in pain from the blow to her stomach. 'We came to see the Serb positions. It would be silly to turn back now just because of a minor incident.'

'Minor incident!' Katy replied. 'That was a minor incident?'

'I think the lady is quite right,' Captain Popović said, indicating Carla. 'There is no point in turning back because some of my men were a bit – how shall we say – confused. Let me accompany you up to see General Dragomir Milošević.'

'You'll come with us and guarantee our safety?' Carla asked.

'Of course. You have my word as a Serb officer and a true lover of my country,' he replied.

'Then we go on,' Carla said in a firm voice, without consulting the others. 'Come on, let's get back into the car.'

A few minutes later they followed Captain Popović's jeep as it moved up the road. Behind them the two army trucks full of soldiers pulled out and followed the journalists' car.

'God, that was scary,' Katy said, looking back at the trucks behind them. She was shaking uncontrollably.

'No. It was not scary,' Haris called from the front. 'Painful yes, scary no.'

'Nonsense!' Carla laughed. 'It was scary all right. And it hurt!' she said, rubbing her stomach where the soldier had hit her.

'Yes, it hurt bad,' Haris said, 'and I think for a moment it is "Goodbye, Katy."'

'Me too,' Katy joined in. 'I'm still shaking.'

'Yes. But what do we do now?' Alberto turned back to them.

'Do?' Katy asked in surprise. 'Do? We follow this Popović fellow up to see General Milošević. For our interviews, newspaper and TV. That's what we've come for. We won't get this opportunity again.'

If anybody did want to turn back they said nothing. In front of them was Popović in his jeep. Behind them were two trucks of inexperienced Serb soldiers. Katy opened her window to let the air flow through the car. 'I'm a survivor!' she told herself. 'I survived, even though for a minute we were in terrible danger.' She suddenly felt strong and confident. Nothing could go wrong now.

Chapter 11 *On a day like this you feel as if you will live forever*

Standing next to the big guns on Mount Trebović, the view over the valley almost took their breath away. The sky was a clear cloudless blue and the sun warmed their backs.

Down below them was the city of Sarajevo. From up here, Katy thought, it looked smaller than you might expect. She could see tall buildings to their right, and over to the left was the main stand of the football stadium. Football had never been one of Katy's main interests, but her brother and his friends were fans. They knew the names of football teams from everywhere, so even she knew about FK Sarajevo, one of the great teams from this part of the world. Once upon a time the stadium below her would have been full of players and chanting fans. She could almost hear the songs, the shouts of excitement and the groans of pain.

No-one played in the stadium any more. No-one played anything any more. And from their position on top of the hill, Sarajevo looked hollow, depressed. There was almost no movement to be seen on its streets, no cars on the ring road, no trains on the railway tracks leading in and out of the city. On a still, windless day like this you might have expected to hear city noises, but there was only a strange silence.

'It is a good position for us, don't you think?' Captain Popović said, indicating Sarajevo with a wave of his hand. 'We can see almost the whole area.'

'Yes. It must be really easy to kill women and children from up here,' Carla said, raising one eyebrow and looking him full in the face.

The captain didn't seem offended, however. Putting his hands into his pockets he looked at them all – the two reporters, the cameraman and Haris, who was still holding his injured mouth. 'Of course,' the captain said, 'we are truly sorry when innocent civilians get caught in this war. We would never make them targets on purpose. But sometimes, in our fight against the Bosnian enemy, against the Croats – against all our enemies – terrible tragedies do happen. War is, after all, a terrible thing.'

A number of questions were running through Katy's brain: exactly who were their enemies? If they fired their big guns into the city from here it was almost impossible not to kill ordinary men, women and children – Bosniaks, Croats, Montenegrins, Slovenians, Serbs – anyone who just happened to be there. And when they'd destroyed Sarajevo, what then? But before she could think of the right question to ask, the captain was speaking again.

'Isn't this a beautiful country?' he was saying with almost boyish enthusiasm. 'On a day like this you feel as if you will live forever. Look over there. What a fantastic view! On a day like this it seems good just to be alive.'

'It *is* good to be alive,' a heavily accented voice behind them shouted. The captain and all the other soldiers stood to attention as a middle-aged man walked up to them. He had small calculating eyes below his cap, a large pistol at his waist and he carried a stick in his right hand. As he approached his face broke into a huge grin and, changing his stick over, he held out his right arm in welcome.

'Welcome in the name of friendship,' he said. 'I am General Dragomir Milošević. And first of all I must apologise for what happened down there.' He pointed back into the valley. 'The men who stopped you – they are not my regular soldiers. They are young hot-blooded Serb men who have joined the struggle for our motherland. But they are new and so far – I have to admit this – they are not well disciplined. But please do not worry. The boys who caused you trouble, they themselves will be in big trouble now. When I, General Dragomir Milošević, do not like something, the people who are responsible have good reason to feel afraid. Now these men …' he indicated all the soldiers who were standing around on the hilltop, 'these men are the regular army. Before they were all in the Yugoslav National Army. Now they serve only Serbia, Greater Serbia, and me, their general.

'Isn't that so, men?' he called, repeating his question, as far as Katy could tell, in Serbo-Croat. A cheer rose up from the men, some of whom had taken off their shirts to make the most of the hot sun. They were so young, so enthusiastic. The scene was very relaxed, almost happy.

'But now,' the general said, after he'd shaken hands with each of them in turn, 'I have talked enough. It is time for you to experience Serb hospitality. Captain Popović, will you please accompany our guests to the camp. It is time, I think, to eat.'

* * *

A few minutes later Katy, Carla, Alberto and Haris were seated at a long table in a tent in the army camp. It was behind the guns under some trees and would be almost impossible to see from the air.

'I didn't expect this,' Carla said to Katy in a quiet voice, as food and drink were brought to them.

'Oh, yes,' the general said, seeing their expressions. 'Everyone helps here, even our female soldiers. Later you can film them. It will show the world what good people we are. It will teach those who criticise us that we too are normal men and women who like to laugh and enjoy ourselves, but that we are prepared to fight for our dream.'

'What exactly is your dream, General?' Katy asked. Before he could answer she went on, 'What I mean is, before all this started, everyone in Yugoslavia lived together in peace. Now suddenly you're killing each other and you say you want to make a new country. Down there …' she pointed back over her shoulder '… people are trying to live their lives and yet you don't want to let them. It doesn't seem like much of a dream to me.'

For a moment the man's smile slipped, and then he raised his glass and took a huge swallow of beer. He wiped his mouth with the back of his hand. He looked at Katy with a mixture of curiosity and hatred. Then his face brightened again and his smile came back.

'Sometimes I wish the world would listen to our story and not believe all the lies which our enemies tell about us. You are young,' he continued, still looking at Katy, 'so perhaps you do not know the history of this part of the world very well. Therefore I will give you a lesson – but before I do, you must understand, you must all of you understand, we Serbs are a peace-loving people. We did not seek this conflict. The Croats started the whole thing. They were killing us. And now those people down there' – he pointed at the city beneath them – 'they want their own independence, and if we let them have that, what will happen to us? Remember our history! Remember our defeat at Kosovo Polje!'

'But that was in the fourteenth century!' Katy said. She'd read about the Ottoman Empire's victory over the Serbs at the Battle of Kosovo in 1389. 'Isn't it time to forget what happened all those years ago?'

'You are wrong. We will never forget what they did to us. If we let them, they will do it again. That is why we are fighting this war. Before, when I was a young man, everything was certain. But now? We are all of us in danger and we have to fight for our people so that we do not get destroyed. That is why Greater Serbia is not just a dream. It is necessary.'

More food and drink was brought for them. The atmosphere became more cheerful as the general and the captain did their best to charm their guests with humorous conversation and repeated explanations of the reasons for this war and how it wasn't their fault. As the hours went by Katy almost began to sympathise with the general's point of view.

In her mind she was already writing her next piece for *The Daily Witness*. She would tell her readers about the history of Yugoslavia, about the Serbs' fears, about the army in the hills. Surely, she thought, Colin would understand. He might not agree, but it was her job to report what the general said. It was her responsibility to inform, to let the world know the story from all its different sides.

At that moment there were three terrific explosions from the direction of the guns. Carla jumped to her feet. 'What was that?' she shouted, as she rushed out of the tent with Katy and Alberto running after her.

'It is nothing for you to worry about,' Captain Popović called after her, as he struggled to his feet. But Carla and Katy weren't listening. With Alberto close behind them, his camera already on his shoulder filming the scene, they made their way towards the guns.

There was a smell of explosives in the evening air. The soldiers were laughing, and pointing down into the valley. Katy and the others followed the direction of their arms. In the city three columns of smoke were rising above the buildings where the shells had landed. Then, to their right, they heard someone shout an order and with a horrible noise two other guns went off, making them jump in surprise. This time they saw the shells land in the city streets. They saw flame and black smoke near the old concert hall. It may have been her imagination, but Katy thought she heard screams in the still air.

The general had come up to them. The soldiers were cheering. He took off his cap and waved it to them. Carla stood there looking down into Sarajevo, her anger burning in her face. She turned round to General Milošević. 'Why did you do that? What was that for?' There was intense anger in her voice.

'It is six o'clock,' the general replied.

'I know it's six o'clock. I have a watch too,' Carla exploded.

'Careful, Carla,' Katy whispered, watching the expression on the general's face. But her friend didn't seem to hear her.

'Six o'clock is the time for the guns,' explained the general. 'You can check it on your watch. I can check it on mine. So we can agree.'

'But why? Who were the guns aiming at?' Carla asked.

'Anybody. Nobody,' the general replied calmly. Alberto's camera swung from Carla to the general.

'But that's inhuman! It's against the rules of war,' Carla shouted.

'Rules of war! We make the rules of war!' said the general. 'We are fighting for our lives. That means the Bosniaks have to leave. Men, women and children. We do not want them in our new motherland. They have to leave all the towns and villages in this area. Go somewhere else. But some of them say they do not want to go. Well, OK. Then we will fight them. It is their decision, not ours. Remember,' he said. 'It is either them or us.'

'But that's ... that's wrong ...' Katy began. The listening soldiers had all gone quiet.

'Perhaps we could go back to the tent and discuss this,' Captain Popović said. 'Some of the things the general has just said, well, they're not exactly what we would like the world to hear. Not like that, anyway.' He sounded very polite, very reasonable.

'I think we've heard quite enough for one day, don't you?' Carla said to Katy, Alberto and Haris, who had left his food to come and join them. 'I think we'd like to go now. Back to Sarajevo. Where anybody is somebody. If that's all right.'

'Well, it is up to you, of course,' the captain said, 'but I would appreciate a few more minutes of your time.'

'I don't—' Carla began, but stopped as a soldier they didn't recognise came up to them.

'Hi, everyone,' said the stranger. 'What's going on here?'

'Meet Jack Hickton,' the captain said, pleased for the interruption.

Katy looked at the man with interest. There was something different about him, as if he didn't really belong here. He had a wide mouth and large eyes which seemed to be smiling directly at her in the evening sun. He carried his gun at his side casually, as if he was just going for a walk, and there was an unlit cigarette hanging from the corner of his mouth. His body was all muscle, hard and fit.

'Hi,' he said, holding out his free hand. 'I'm Jack Hickton. From New York. Not quite what you expected, huh?'

'Yes. No,' Katy replied, trying not to embarrass herself. 'What are you doing here?'

'I'm just here for the party, you might say,' the handsome soldier replied.

'Party?' she said stupidly. Carla and Alberto had moved away with Haris and were talking to Captain Popović.

'OK, I'll be honest with you. I'm here for the money – and the fun!' He was laughing at her.

'You're a mercenary? You're doing this for money?' Katy asked.

'Well, I like to call myself a professional soldier. It sounds better,' he said.

'Yes, but it's the same thing, isn't it?' she said.

'Yes, I guess it is. But I'm not really bothered, to tell the truth.' He was looking at her with a smile. 'What about you? I guess you're a journalist?' he went on.

Katy nodded.

'I tell you what,' the American said. 'Why don't you spend the day with me tomorrow?'

'Spend the day with you?' What was he suggesting?

'Yeah. I'll take you round the city. Show you what's *really* going on.'

'But I—' she protested.

'No buts.' Jack Hickton laughed. 'You can see what a professional soldier like me does. It would make a good story for your newspaper. What do you say?'

'Yes, all right,' she said, deciding quickly. 'That might be a good idea.'

* * *

When Katy, Carla and the others left to drive back down to Sarajevo, Captain Popović sent a group of soldiers to protect them. Despite Carla's anger and the argument which had followed with the general, the captain had remained polite and calm. He'd insisted on telling them again and again about Croat aggression and the threat to the Serbs in Bosnia. He was clearly educated and cultured. What was it, Katy asked herself, about nations and tribes that changed a man like that? Years from now, if he survived, how would he explain himself to his children? Perhaps Captain Popović was just one more victim of war – a man ruined by circumstance.

She had time to think about all this on the drive back because no-one talked very much. And then, when they got back to the hotel, it was quite late and Katy didn't feel like going to the bar, so she said goodnight quickly and went to her room.

But why, she thought to herself as she slipped into bed, hadn't she told her friends about her arrangement to meet the American soldier tomorrow? 'It's because it's wrong,' she told herself as she started to fade into sleep. 'There's something wrong with it. I'll tell him I've changed my mind. I won't go with him.'

Chapter 12   *Katy's dream*

She was in a boat on a lake. The sun was shining and there were small white clouds in the sky. She was sitting next to her mother at the back of the boat, trailing her hand in the cool water. Her father was rowing them across the lake with a smile on his face, his hat pushed back on his head. Katy was so happy to have him back again after all these years. She looked up into her mother's face to see if she was happy too, but the woman next to her wasn't her mother. It was Carla, laughing at her. She splashed some lake water in Katy's face. Katy laughed back at her. 'See,' Carla said. 'Look around you! We're on a lake with sides, many sides. We have to tell all sides of our story.' Katy looked around her. On one bank there was a city, on another the mountains, on another a beautiful park with music and sunshine.

'No. There's only one side,' Katy's father said, pushing his hat further back. 'Only one side.' She looked out of the boat and now, suddenly, it was true. The lake had become a sea and they were far from the shore. She was frightened. The water was grey and the clouds weren't clouds any more. They were the bursts of gunfire in the air. It started to rain. 'Father!' she called. 'Father, help! Get us back to the shore.'

Her father was rowing them across the sea. Except that it wasn't her father now, it was Dragomir Milošević, the general, and his laughter was cold and ugly. 'All right,' he said, resting on his oars as the boat rose and fell in the stormy sea. 'I will help you, but you have to help me first.'

'Of course,' she said. She was really afraid now. 'What do you want me to do?'

'Help me kill them,' he said, pointing to the shore. It was closer now and she could see people waving at her – Haris, Colin, Carla's friends Vlada and Imrana, Nataša and her children. They were all shouting at her in friendship. Then she heard a beautiful sound – music, the high notes of a saxophone coming across the water – and she saw Željko, the tall dark-haired Željko. He was playing just for her. And her father, who wasn't really her father, but the general, said, 'It is six o'clock. It is time to kill nobody.' She looked over to her friends on the shore, but they had turned their backs. And the little boat was sinking and she was screaming, 'No, no, don't leave me, please don't leave me!' though whether she was shouting to the people on the shore or the person who wasn't her father it was impossible to tell. The saxophone played on. And then she heard the sound of distant gunfire, only this time it was real and she woke up.

* * *

Katy had overslept and it was midday when she went downstairs. She was walking across the hotel lobby trying to get her dream out of her head, when she heard her name.

'Katy! Katy Sullivan!' It was Jack Hickton, the American mercenary. He was dressed in jeans and a dark T-shirt and was carrying a large rucksack. 'You coming with me?' he asked.

'No, I … I don't think …' she started, remembering the decision she had made the night before.

'Hey come on! Remember, I said I'd show you stuff. Think of the great story you'll get out of it! Pulitzer prize at least!'

* * *

'What do you do in the city?' she shouted above the noise of the jeep's engine as they roared through the streets.

'Anything they ask me,' he shouted back. 'I mostly see if I can find any Bosnian soldiers.'

'What happens when you do?' she asked. She wanted to know how he would reply.

'Well then,' he laughed at her, 'well then, I guess I have to try and kill them before they kill me.'

'And have you?' she asked.

'Have I what?'

'Killed any of them?' she asked.

'A few.' Then seeing her face he said, 'Hey lady, that's what I do. That's war. You sure you want to come with me?'

She nearly said no. But she was a reporter. This was real. She would be able to write about it: 'My day with the mercenary'. She could mix it in with the piece about the guns on the hills.

And so, even though at the back of her mind she knew – just as she had last night – that she was getting in deeper than she wanted, she let her desire for a good story and a bit of excitement get the better of her anxiety.

Jack Hickton drove her round the city. He drove as fast and as crazily as Haris, only, she thought, better. In mid-afternoon he stopped the jeep. He got some sandwiches from his pack and offered her one. She ate it gratefully. He gave her a can of beer. It was hot. She drank it. He offered her some pills. 'Uppers,' he told her. 'They help me concentrate. Keep me on my toes.' But Katy had never been into drugs, so she said no. 'Suit yourself,' the soldier said, before swallowing three of the pills with his beer.

Later they left the jeep by the side of the road. 'We have to go on foot from here,' he told her. They started towards some buildings on the side of a hill. Before the war the area had been full of luxury homes and the occasional hotel. Now it was the same empty mess as the rest of the city.

They came to a tall building. 'This used to be quite a good hotel,' he said. 'Not much of a place now, is it?' They walked through the entrance. It was deserted. There was no glass in the windows, but there was glass on the floor mixed with papers and empty suitcases. There was no electricity, and so, in the heat of the late afternoon, they climbed the stairs. Ahead of Katy, the American almost ran and she followed him with difficulty, her breath coming in great gasps.

Finally he stopped. 'I reckon this is far enough,' he said. 'The fifteenth floor.' He was sweating and his large blue eyes were hard. His smile wasn't friendly any more. It was cruel, like a crazy animal. She should have gone then. But still she didn't. There was something so real about her day, and Jack Hickton would make such a terrific story. She was sure of it.

They went into a bedroom and he put down his rucksack. He looked out of the window, down onto the street, down onto a dirt track. He pointed to two little girls running, carrying a plastic can full of water.

Jack Hickton, professional soldier, animal-crazy with the drugs he'd taken – or maybe just mad-crazy anyway and she hadn't noticed because she was after a good story – asked her which of the two little girls he should kill. And because it was a decision no human being should be asked to make, she refused to say, so he shot them both. He seemed to enjoy it. But for Katy it was the end of everything she'd ever believed in and she felt sick and angry and hopeless. But then, just as in her dream, she heard the high sad sound of a solo saxophone in the distance, calling out over the suffering city.

Chapter 13 *Sally and Joanna*

She was running along the street, running away from the terror, her heart nearly exploding with fear and horror. She couldn't stop the tears which fell from her eyes, or the cries which poured from her mouth. She tried to look around her as she ran, but all she could see were the two little girls, dead in the hot dust. She stopped and wiped her eyes. She tried to put the dead children out of her mind, but they just wouldn't go away.

The streets were deserted in the warm evening air. Nobody seemed to be moving anywhere. The only sound was the occasional cry of a bird. It is a curious thing, Colin had told her, but you get a lot of birds in a war. She didn't know where she was. Ever since she'd left the hotel she'd been running, running anywhere to get away from the soldier who had murdered the girls far below him, the soldier who had laughed, who had got her involved. Now she was out of breath. She pulled the scarf from round her neck and wiped her eyes again. She tried to dry the sweat that was running down her face. She bent down to get her breath back. She looked around her trying to work out where she was.

A huge explosion about six blocks away made her stand up straight again. She felt the ground shake and saw the flames and smoke rise above the buildings to her left. Then a bullet whizzed through the air, hitting the door of a house behind her. Oh, God. A sniper. Another sniper. Maybe it was the crazy American. Now he was going to kill her too. She didn't want to die. Not yet.

She began to run again, away from the smoke of the explosion. Another bullet whizzed past her head. And another. Without thinking she turned down a side street, running away from the noise and the danger. Her mind was completely empty now. She'd stopped crying. She'd stopped thinking. All she knew was that she had to keep going.

She heard the sound of an engine behind her. It sounded like a motorbike, a small motorbike. She ran faster, but the motorbike, or whatever it was, was going faster than she was. It was getting closer and closer. She tried to get away, but she couldn't. The motorbike was right behind her. Now it was passing her. It had passed her. She didn't look at it. She stopped and tried to decide where to run next. In front of her someone was shouting. She waited for the bullet that would kill her. She didn't care any more. It didn't matter. Nothing mattered.

The man in front of her was shouting louder. Gradually she realised that he'd changed to English.

'You come,' he was saying. 'You come quick. You want die? Come quick.' She raised her head. A thin white-haired man was sitting on an old moped, trying to get her to join him.

'Quick,' he kept saying, 'quick before guns!' He looked up at the buildings around them. 'Quick!' he shouted one more time, 'or I go. Leave you.'

Katy woke up suddenly and rushed towards him. She sat behind him on the old moped and he roared off down the street.

'Where you go?' he called back to her.

She shouted the name of her hotel. He nodded without speaking and they continued at top speed. He drove from side to side across the street. She was sure she would fall off.

He turned back again. '*Novinar?*' he shouted. 'Journalist?'

'Yes,' she said.

'Good,' he replied, 'very good,' though what he thought was good she didn't know. The engine roared. He raced across the dead frightened city. They didn't speak again. And then suddenly they were outside her hotel with all its lights on, in the one part of the city that was safe. She got off the moped, but even before she could ask him who he was – or thank him for saving her life – he'd disappeared into the night.

She ran in through the hotel doors, past the reception desk, past the lifts and straight into the bar and there, thank God, was Colin.

When he saw her coming he jumped to his feet and ran to her. He put his arms around her and pulled her to him. 'Katy!' he said. 'I thought you were … we thought you were …'

'Colin,' she cried, 'Colin,' repeating his name over and over again.

'It's OK, it's OK. You're safe now,' he said.

'Oh, God, Colin, what have I done?' she said through her tears.

'Calm down. What is it? What's the matter?' he asked.

'I've just done something terrible. Children. Two little children. He wanted me to choose, and I didn't, and now they're both dead.' The words were pouring out of her mouth, and although she didn't want to, she started to cry again. Colin bought her a brandy, and then another, and soon she'd calmed down enough to tell him what it was all about. About the ruined hotel, and the crazy American, and the two little children lying in the Sarajevo dirt.

'Why on earth did you arrange to meet him? Why did you go with him?' They were sitting at the bar. Some of the other journalists were listening. Colin was watching her with a worried look on his face. The moment he finished his cigarette, he lit another one.

'I thought … I thought it would be something I could write about,' Katy said.

'It is,' Colin said.

'How? How can I?' she cried. 'I was a part of it. I was there. He made me a part of it. He's crazy. He's disgusting. What am I going to do?'

'I did warn you, didn't I?' Colin didn't sound angry. He sounded desperately sad.

'Yes. And I didn't listen because I wanted to do this job well. But now? Who cares about the job! Oh, God! I just keep making mistakes.'

'No, you don't. You just keep learning, that's all. And if you have the courage, you can write about this and you can tell your readers how easy it is to be drawn in, to get involved, so that you become a part of a story you're supposed to be telling them all about.'

'I feel so stupid,' Katy said.

'I don't think your readers will see it that way. You didn't pull the trigger, did you?' Colin argued.

'Yes, but if I hadn't gone with him …' She couldn't finish the thought.

'But you did. It happened. In this terrible city it's already the past. Now it's the future that matters. Now you must start thinking about the future, what you can do about the future. You can't be objective now, can you? You can't be *fair* about this. You can't put your soldier's side of the argument, can you? There is no side now, no good reason for what you've just seen. Now you've only got one choice. You've got to tell people what's *really* happening here. We all have to. Again and again. Until they believe us. Until the whole world gets so angry about what's happening here that they wake up and do something about it. Until ordinary people get so cross that they hammer at the doors of all the leaders until finally, before it's too late, the big powers – America, Russia, Europe – come in here and stop this awful killing. This is it, Katy. You've seen enough. Use your strength. Use your power. Mix that with the anger you're feeling now and you can really achieve something.' He was red in the face.

Katy got off her stool and turned to go. There was a mad look in her eyes. She headed for the door.

'Katy,' he called, 'wait. There's something I haven't told you. There's something you should know.' But she didn't hear him as she rushed out of the bar towards the lifts. Colin got up and started to follow her. Then he stopped and lowered his head. He ran his fingers through his hair. When he looked up there were tears in his eyes. He went back to the bar.

* * *

In her room Katy switched on the light and went straight to her computer and started it up without even bothering to lock the door behind her. She began to type, biting her lower lip as she concentrated on what she wanted to say.

JUST LIKE YOUR CHILDREN

This is a story of two children. Let's imagine that they're nine years old. We'll call them Sally and Joanna. They're just like your children, but there are some differences I'd like to tell you about.

Let's imagine that Sally and Joanna live in an apartment block. Their front doors are opposite each other. When they can, they play together, but unlike your children they don't go to school because there are no schools any more. Many of the teachers have left. Some have died. And the risk of an enemy shell landing on a crowded classroom and killing everyone – children and teachers alike – is too great.

Sally and Joanna are much older than their nine years. They have seen too much death for children of their age. They live with their mothers and brothers, sisters, aunts and grandmothers. You can be sure that their fathers aren't at home. They've gone to war to protect their families. They're probably dead.

There's no electricity in the apartment building, so the families have to use candles and old oil lamps. There's no running water either, so every day the two girls get a plastic can and take it to the centre of the city where a water pipe is working. They fill the can and then they carry it, running as fast as they can, back to the apartment block where their mothers are waiting.

Sally and Joanna run because they're afraid. To get from their apartment block to the water pipe they have to go along a dusty track by the railway. People here call it 'Sniper Alley' because in the tall buildings on either side, soldiers sit with powerful rifles fitted with telescopic sights. They shoot anything that moves just like you would shoot rabbits. They like shooting children especially because children are smaller – more difficult to hit. When you hit a child it shows that you're a very good shot.

Earlier today a young soldier, an American mercenary, shot Sally and Joanna, children just like yours. I watched him do it. God forgive me, I thought I was covering a good news story. He laughed as he shot them, two children, trying to get water for their mothers.

Sally and Joanna are dead. We can't do anything for them any more. But unless people do something, and do something soon, there will be many more Sallys and Joannas, little children whose only crime was to be alive in the wrong place, in a bitter, senseless war.

If, like me, you can't bear this story, make time to do something about it. Write to politicians, write to the United Nations, protest in the streets, write to anyone you can think of. Tell them Sally and Joanna are dead and tell them it's time this was made to stop.

The first rule of journalism Katy had learnt was that you never send anything to the paper until you've read it once, twice, three times. But tonight she didn't worry about that. She connected the satellite phone, dialled the number and sent the article on its way to *The Daily Witness*. And when she'd done that she didn't even bother to look at the email messages waiting for her. She just switched off the computer and lay down on her bed, covering her eyes to try and stop herself seeing, again and again, the little bodies, the arm moving, waving a last goodbye.

Chapter 14 *Red eyes*

She must have fallen asleep. But not for long. There was a loud knocking at the door. She got up and opened it. Carla was standing in the corridor with two bottles of wine in her hand. She was crying.

'Carla!' Katy said in astonishment. 'What's the matter?' Carla wasn't the sort of person who cried.

'Everything's the matter,' Carla said, walking into the room. 'Drink with me.' She went to the bathroom and came back with two plastic glasses. She poured the wine and handed one glass to Katy. 'Drink!' she commanded through her tears.

'Why? What for?' The woman in front of her was so unlike the Carla that Katy knew. She was suddenly afraid.

'We'll drink to Vlada and Imrana and the others. Because we have failed. Because we did nothing for them and now there's nothing to be done. Oh, my God,' she cried, falling onto the bed and pouring her wine all over the floor.

'Carla, what's happened?' Katy asked.

Carla got up and poured herself another glass. She lit a cigarette and went to stand by the window. When she turned back her tears had stopped and her face was suddenly white and blank. 'You remember the guns,' she said, 'at six o'clock. Up there on the mountain. You remember?'

'Of course I remember,' Katy replied.

'Well, one of them, two of them, I don't know … We saw them … the music … Vlada, Imrana …' She stopped speaking. For a second Katy thought she had stopped breathing. Then she lifted her head and in an expressionless voice said, 'The shells landed next to the steps of the old concert hall. The shells exploded in the crowd at Željko's concert. They'd just started playing. And sixteen people, innocent people, died in seconds. My friends, Vlada and Imrana. And two of the saxophonists, killed, just like that.'

'Željko?' Katy couldn't stop herself. 'What about Željko?'

'I think he survived,' Carla said. 'That's what I heard. But I don't know.'

* * *

Katy woke up early the next morning. The sky beyond the hotel window was still grey. There was silence all around. No voices. No traffic. No guns. She realised that she was still dressed although she was under the bed covers. She had a terrible headache. The room smelt of cigarette smoke.

She managed to get out of bed, take off her clothes and go into the bathroom. The water was hot and made her feel slightly better. Afterwards she put on a clean pair of jeans and a blue shirt. She stood blankly at the window and watched the sky gradually getting lighter over the quiet city. Without really thinking she switched on her laptop and read the emails that were waiting for her. One of them was from her friend Benjamin. She read it, but without interest.

Hi
I hope this won't come as an unpleasant shock, but I've betrayed you! Yes, that's it. I've actually gone off with someone else. In fact I've moved in with her. Millie. A lawyer. You'll really like her, I know you will. How are you out there? Please stay safe. Will you ever forgive me?!
Your ex-would-be-lover Benjamin

Another was from Caryl Jones.

Your piece about the girls was really excellent. It's on our front page today. Keep up the good work.
Caryl

Still moving automatically, without thinking or feeling, she switched off her computer, left her room and walked to the lift. When she got to the dining room it was empty except for one figure seated in the far corner with her back towards her.

'My God,' Carla said to her when Katy tapped her on the shoulder. 'You look terrible.'

'So do you,' Katy said, 'although with those dark glasses it's difficult to be sure.'

'I didn't sleep at all last night after I left you. I don't want people to see my eyes.' Red eyes. Red from weeping.

Katy sat down opposite her friend. Then she stood up. Then she sat down again. There was something she had to do if only she could think straight. But her mind was still full of guns and children, rifle shots and music. Music! Suddenly she knew. She got up.

'Where are you going?' Carla asked. 'They haven't even started serving breakfast yet.'

'I don't want breakfast!'

'It'll do you good. We have to go on, you know. We have a job to do. That's why we're here.' She was trying hard to be the old Carla again, not the Carla from a few hours before.

'I don't care about my job,' Katy said. 'I've got to find him.'

'Find who? What are you talking about? '

'Željko,' Katy said, the name almost a cry, and she ran out of the room.

Chapter 15 *Music*

Katy searched for Željko all day. No-one seemed to know where he was – or if they did they wouldn't tell her. She went from the hotel to the basement where he used to play. But it was deserted. She went to the park, and from there to the part of town where Nataša lived. Once she heard the sound of gunfire and saw a puff of smoke from a building to her right. On other occasions she thought she felt bullets pass by her as snipers tried to shoot her down, but in her confused state she couldn't be sure whether she was imagining it. Her head was full of strange and terrible pictures – of the little girls, of bombs and music, the crash of guns in the hills. She kept seeing Željko's face in front of her, his expression changed forever by the terrible things that had happened as his city lived, day after day, in pain.

Around midday she arrived at the market, which was still functioning despite the danger and yesterday's killing. It was only when she saw the tables with their small tired collections of fruit and vegetables that she realised that she hadn't eaten. She bought an apple and some carrots, which she ate right there in front of the surprised market trader – though for him nothing was really strange any more. At the side street café where she'd once eaten with Carla and Haris she had a beer, which made her head feel even lighter. She asked for some bread or a biscuit, but there was nothing to eat in the café. In the end she had a coffee after her beer. She filled it with sugar to give her energy.

After a few minutes she realised that the woman who worked there was watching her. That wasn't surprising; she was the only customer. Katy smiled and the woman smiled back. Katy finished her coffee. The woman smiled again and nodded her head.

'It's good coffee,' Katy said. She felt she had to say something.

'Journalist?' the woman asked.

'Yes,' Katy said.

'Good coffee,' the woman said. 'Difficult to find.'

'Yes,' Katy said, and then, because it was all she was thinking about, 'Željko? Where is Željko? Do you know where Željko is?'

'Željko,' the woman said slowly, '*muzičkih.*'

'Yes, that's right. Music. Željko,' Katy said.

'Six.' The woman held up six fingers and pointed at her watch. Then she told her where she could find him and Katy wondered why she hadn't thought of it before.

* * *

Six o'clock. The afternoon sun was beginning to fade. Katy heard him before she saw him. It was the same sad solo saxophone, high and beautiful, playing a tune that rose up and up until it seemed it could go no higher – and then it started again, the same extraordinary melody, climbing, rising into the evening sky, like a gentle sorrowful sigh.

He was standing on the ruins of the steps of the old concert hall. In front of him there was a huge hole in the street and she could see terrible dark stains, the blood of the people killed and wounded in the concert explosion.

Željko was wearing the clothes of a classical musician: black tailcoat, white shirt, white bow tie. His saxophone case was by his side. He was standing straight as he played. For some reason Katy was reminded of church. A small crowd of people was standing in the street, sheltering in doorways.

Željko stopped playing and at that moment there was the thump of two explosions somewhere to the south. The people ran, disappearing into the streets by the park. Now only the two of them were left as he put his saxophone into its case. He looked up and noticed her, and for a long moment their eyes met as they looked at each other. Finally she spoke.

'What are you doing? What are you doing here?' Though she knew the answer already.

'I was playing for my friends,' Željko said.

'I heard you yesterday.' For a moment she was back in that hotel bedroom. 'Were you playing for your friends then?'

'Yes,' he replied.

'You're going to play for them every day?' she asked.

'Sixteen people died here two days ago. Musicians, friends, ordinary people. They were listening to music. What is wrong with that? Tell me, what is wrong with that?'

'Nothing. Nothing at all,' Katy said softly.

'Sixteen people. Sixteen days. Each day a different person. I have fourteen more days.' He spoke as if what he was saying was the most obvious thing in the world.

'But Željko, it's dangerous. You'll get killed. A sniper. A shell from the hills.' Her words sounded ridiculous in the middle of the ruined street.

'So what?' he said.

'Please don't say that.' She had to try and reach him somehow.

'It is all there is to say. I have to play for my friends. To say goodbye,' he said.

'What was it, the tune?' she asked. 'It's beautiful.'

'It is my version of a song by the German composer Richard Strauss. He wrote it near the end of his life. One of his "Four Last Songs". In German it is called *"Beim Schlafengehen"*, in English something like "On going to sleep". The words say that the tired spirit should have a happy restful journey at the end of a long life – as the person goes to that perfect endless sleep where it may "live deeply". My girlfriend – a girl I knew in London,' he corrected himself quickly, 'sang it in a competition at the Academy of Music. She won the competition. That was a life ago, a different world. But the melody – it is the right tune for this place, I think.' He looked around him and his eyes filled with tears.

Katy rushed up the steps and put her arms around him. 'Željko,' she whispered. 'Poor, dear Željko. Let me help you.'

For a moment he said nothing. Then he raised his head and gently removed Katy's arms from around him.

'Come,' he said, picking up his saxophone case, 'and I will show you what we have lost.' He took her hand and led her up the steps and in through the empty doorway at the front of the building – the entrance to the concert hall.

Inside the damaged building they walked down what had once been corridors, and then they were suddenly in a large empty space, big enough for hundreds of people. She could see the sky through the remains of the roof. There were broken chairs, and the floor was covered in rubbish – the mess that war leaves.

'That is where I used to play when I was at the university.'

He pointed to the stage, open to the sky. 'I was lucky. I was principal clarinet in the university orchestra for two years.'

Katy tried to imagine the concert hall full of people and musicians. For just a second she could smell the perfume, hear the audience talking excitedly before the conductor walked onto the stage. Applause. He raises his arms. Music.

'Come,' Željko said. 'I will show you where we used to practise.' He led her to a side room. He looked around the room, as if seeing his old colleagues again. Then he lowered his head and covered his eyes with his hands.

'Željko,' she said quietly, seeing his shoulders shaking. 'Željko,' she said again, going over to him and putting her arms around him as she had done outside on the steps. This time he didn't pull away from her. He started to cry, a terrible sound, hard and bitter in the silence all around them. She held him tight, and then later, when he'd stopped, she lifted her face to his and kissed his sad eyes, touched his sweet mouth, ran her fingers through his thick hair. For a moment he didn't react, but then, when she felt him respond, when she felt his strong hands reach for her body, she didn't resist.

The evening turned into night, but they stayed there as the bright moon rose into the dark sky and shone down upon them. All around them was the terrible silence of fear, but they ignored it as she comforted him, holding him close to her, in the empty room of a building that had once been full of music. And then, as if it was the most natural thing in the world, they were making love, and for a long still moment she forgot the terrible things she'd seen and she felt him forget the past and the future too, and their cries of joy were cries of peace.

In the morning as it got light she said, 'I love you, Željko.'

'No, you do not,' he said gently.

'Yes, I do. I love what you are, what you're doing. It's the most beautiful thing I've ever seen, the most beautiful thing I've ever heard.'

'No,' he said, 'it is not beautiful. It is necessary. It is not me that you love, it is the language I speak, the language that we all speak. It is the music which speaks to you, the music which says that death is not here, that the people – my friends, those people at the concert, the mothers and the children – that they are here, still here. Still here with us now.'

Suddenly, as she buttoned her shirt, she felt like a stranger, as if they'd just met. He turned to her and took her face in his strong hands, his beautiful fingers.

'I am sorry, Katy. I can tell you these things and you can understand them, because you are kind and intelligent and beautiful and lovely. But you cannot feel the experience as I do. Your ghosts do not live here, but mine do.' He was looking past her now, his dark eyes searching far away for a place that she couldn't see. He took his hands from her face. It was over.

'I'm going to write about you, you know,' she told him.

'If that is what you want,' he replied.

'Yes, it is.' And when she got back to the hotel, and when she'd told an anxious Colin that she was safe and that she was sorry he'd been worried about her, she went straight up to her room, a sad smile on her face, and her next article flowed out of her like love.

MUSIC

I haven't had much success in love so far. A few boyfriends, nothing serious. And then recently I had a partner and I thought he was 'Mr Right', but he wasn't. He didn't think he was, anyway. Then I came to Sarajevo.

You probably think that I shouldn't be telling you this in a newspaper report from a war zone. Love has a hard time when there's so much death around. But I'm going to tell you about Željko Kojić and what he is and does. So I have to tell you about me because I love him.

I love Željko Kojić because of his beautiful music. I love him because he plays the saxophone like a poet. I love him because he is fantastically brave. But most of all I love him because here, in this city of despair, he is a symbol of hope and because here, where children die every day, he teaches people how to live.

Two days ago Željko organised one of the concerts I have written about before. People went to the steps of the old concert hall to hear him and his friends play for them. They were looking forward to an evening of happiness in the middle of horror. Then a shell from one of the big guns landed and sixteen people were killed. They were ordinary people like you and me, shopkeepers and housewives, teachers and students, taxi drivers and nurses, and musicians. They were Bosniaks and Croats and Serbs (yes, because there are many Serbs here who love this city and hate what's being done in their name). They were the good people, who look beyond their race and background and see their brothers and sisters, not 'others'. But they died because up there, in the hills beyond the city, there are people who aren't like them at all and who don't care who they kill in their insane desire for some kind of final solution.

Željko Kojić didn't die that evening, but something in his soul died. Except music, the only thing he has left. And so every day, at six o'clock, he goes to the place where the shell landed. He goes at six o'clock because that's exactly the time those sixteen people died. He will stand there in the sunshine or the rain and play a piece of music by Richard Strauss, 'On going to sleep'. In his hands it's a melody full of regret and sadness, and if I was a better writer I could describe it to you. The best thing I can say is that when you hear it you know what it is to lose everything and, at the same time, you know how wonderful it is to be alive.

And so for sixteen days from the terrible day those sixteen people died, Željko will stand and play his saxophone. Snipers will shoot at him and shells will land in the street near him. But I know, in the fourteen days remaining, that he will live and that his music will float over this tragic city. I don't know how I know this, but I believe it to be true. What he's doing is the best thing I have experienced here, perhaps anywhere. His saxophone cries for the people in this city, for the dead and the living. It cries to the monsters in the hills, telling them to stop. It cries out to all of us.

Now I ask myself how beauty and ugliness can live together in this terrible place and I wonder which will win. And I ask you, who read this article, how long it will take for you to hear Željko's music. Because when you do you will, like me, know that something, anything has to be done, now, to stop the killing and let life start again.

Chapter 16 *A song for the living*

'What is it about war reporters that makes us so strange?' Carla asked.

They were sitting in the bar, waiting. It was late afternoon. They were drinking the first beers of the day, but Colin, for some reason, was having orange juice.

'It's the excitement,' a man from an American TV station said.

'Excitement?' Katy asked.

'Yeah. The knowledge of danger. It's addictive. Like a drug,' said the man. 'After you've done it once, you have to have the experience again and again. Some people climb mountains. Me, I report wars. And it's important. We're important. It's a special job, telling the truth. Put all that together and it's something you just have to do. The best job in the world. The worst.'

'Not much good for real life, marriages, partners, children,' Colin said.

'Yeah,' said the American, 'that's a problem. I'm divorced.' He looked over at Katy invitingly. 'Single. But then so are most of us – Colin over there, Alberto, the guys from the British papers. Well, one of them said he was going to try and save his marriage – Ed Jonas. You're the only one who seems to be able to stay with your husband, Carla.'

'That's because I'm a woman. No, no, I'm joking. Don't look so angry. It's difficult. Of course it is,' the Italian replied.

'I heard some news from Ed Jonas,' Katy interrupted.

'You did? How is he?' Colin said.

'Much better. A colleague, a friend of mine at *The Daily Witness*, sent me an email. He's got back together with his wife, just as he hoped, and he isn't nearly as ill as he thought. He's expecting to get better. And he's become a grandfather now too. So you should all stop being so depressed. You don't have to mess up everything just because you're in this job!'

'Listen to her,' said another newsman. 'She thinks she's got all the answers.'

'No, I don't,' Katy protested. 'It's just—'

'Oh, come on,' Alberto said. It was the first time he'd said anything during these conversations. 'That's all unimportant. Today is the day, isn't it? When the outside world stops this dreadful bloodshed. At last.'

That's what they were waiting for. It was almost two weeks since Katy had found Željko outside the ruins of the old concert hall. A week ago there'd been yet another attack – shells on the market place, which had killed another thirty-seven people and wounded many more. Finally, it seemed as if the rest of the world had woken up, especially after Serb troops had raided a United Nations post. The Americans had told the Serbs to stop shelling the city. The Serbs had said it was none of the Americans' business. But the Americans had said yes, it was, and if the Serbs didn't stop killing civilians in Sarajevo they would send in their planes and destroy the Serb guns. The Serbs didn't stop. The American ultimatum had another thirty minutes left.

'Come on,' a Canadian journalist said. 'Let's get up on the roof and see what happens.'

They all left the bar and headed for the lifts, but at that moment there was another power cut and they had to walk up sixteen floors. As they opened the door and stepped out into the late-afternoon sunshine, Carla stopped Katy and took her to one side.

'What is it?' Katy asked. For one terrible moment she thought it might be bad news about Željko. Although she hadn't talked to him since their night together, she'd watched him playing almost every day at six o'clock, and he'd seen her and smiled at her. He was always in her thoughts.

But it wasn't about Željko.

'I wanted to tell you something,' her Italian friend said, 'about Colin.'

'Colin?' Katy repeated.

'Yes. Did you know that he'd lost his job?' Carla asked.

'No,' Katy said. 'Why? When?'

'He decided that he didn't want to film wars any more. He's had enough of death and killing. That's what he told his boss. So they said OK and sacked him.'

'Oh, no. When was this?'

'A week ago.'

'A week ago? Why is he still here then?' Katy asked.

'Are you blind, Katy? He stayed because of you.'

'Because of me?' Katy had been aware of Colin's growing affection for her over the weeks – after their first misunderstanding. But her Italian friend was exaggerating, surely. She looked over at the cameraman. He smiled back at her, and suddenly she knew that Carla was right.

'My God,' Carla cried. 'Look!' Katy followed her pointing arm to the puffs of smoke where the shells landed, and a second later they heard the noise of the guns on the mountain.

'It's the hospital. They're shelling the hospital,' Carla cried. They ran towards the others.

'Get down!' Colin said. 'We're not safe here. They're firing everywhere.'

It was true. The air was suddenly full of explosions and sniper fire. The two women got down, hiding behind the wall. 'The Americans will have to come now,' Carla said.

'Yes, but it's too late, isn't it? Too late for the people of Sarajevo,' Alberto said. He was balancing his camera on his shoulder.

'It's never too late – where there's hope,' Carla said.

'It's sad, isn't it?' Colin was shouting above the noise of gunfire. 'If they stop, it'll be because someone is stronger than they are. Not because they understand. Not because they want to stop. And the worst thing is that if only the Americans or the Europeans or somebody had done something like this months ago, hundreds of people wouldn't have been killed.'

'They don't seem to be very frightened of the Americans,' Carla shouted.

'That's just because they want to kill as many people as possible before the Americans come,' Katy said. 'If they can empty the city of Bosniaks and Croats and anyone else who happens to be around, they can come in and take the city over when peace arrives.'

'Look!' Alberto shouted, pointing behind him. 'Look up there!'

They turned and looked up into the sky. Three American war planes were screaming towards them. As they watched the planes separated and flew in different directions. There were bursts of flame and smoke as they fired their rockets. Then, for the first time since she'd been here, Katy saw a different kind of explosion in the hills. This time it wasn't the guns firing; the guns themselves were being destroyed.

One of the planes flashed over the roof. It was so low you could almost touch it. The American markings were clearly visible. The noise was terrible. The reporters covered their ears. There were more explosions in the hills. And then the planes were gone. The whole attack had lasted less than five minutes.

Katy looked at her watch. It was nearly six o'clock in the afternoon and something wasn't right. She looked at the others. She saw it in their eyes too. They were all wondering what was different. Then she realised what it was. Silence, a still moment, as if the world had stopped turning. They heard a bird sing, and then coming up to them on the wind a song, played on a solo saxophone. Željko's song, on the sixteenth day – a song for the ghosts, a song for the living.

'Listen,' Katy said, jumping to her feet. 'Listen, it's Željko. It's Željko. Playing his song. Maybe it really is over.'

She felt the bullets hammer into her just before she heard two rifle shots from a nearby building. She was knocked backwards onto the concrete roof. She heard Colin shouting, and later Carla's voice next to her ear saying, 'Are you all right, Katy? Speak to me, Katy.' But the voices were faint and getting fainter and further away. Now she could hardly hear them. Suddenly it was dark and she felt as if she was going to sleep, going home, and then there was only silence. And then there was nothing.

Coda   *Footsteps*

The sound of footsteps down a corridor. Flashes of light. She tries to open her eyes. The crash of metal. Voices. Voices. A familiar voice. Who is it? She can't think. She can't think at all. She hears her name. Is that her name? She hears the sound of wheels. If only she could open her eyes. But the voices disappear, the light goes and she sinks back into blackness.

* * *

'Is she any better?'

'Nothing has changed, Mrs Sullivan.' A man's voice. She doesn't recognise it.

'But if she never comes round? If she never wakes up?' Her mother is talking. She sounds upset.

'I'm afraid there's nothing we can do, Mrs Sullivan. We just have to wait.'

'How are you going to tell her? If – I mean when – she wakes up?' Her brother's voice!

'I wish she'd wake up. Please, Katy.' It *is* her brother.

She tries to open her eyes. She makes a huge effort. She wants to say, 'I'm awake,' and 'Tell me what?' Most of all she wants to know what her mother and her brother are doing here. She listens to her mother crying.

She tries to speak, but she can't make any words.

'What's that? Katy! Did you say something? I think she's trying to say something.' But the voices fade again and she drifts away into blackness.

* * *

Much, much later she opens her eyes. She's in a strange room with white walls, a large window, the sound of traffic. There are flowers all around her.

'Katy,' her mother says. 'Oh, Katy, are you all right?'

'Mum! Where am I?'

'You're in a hospital in London. You were shot. You've been very ill. You've been unconscious for weeks. But you're better now.' She holds Katy's hand. Katy closes her eyes.

* * *

Later, when she wakes up again, Colin is there.

'Colin? What are you doing here?'

'I just came to see how you were. Well, I've been here a few days actually.'

'Oh, Colin. It's nice to see you. My mother was here. And my brother.'

'Yes. They've been here every day since you were brought to London. I told them to go home for a sleep. I said I would stay with you for a bit.'

'How is everybody? How's Carla? What's happening in Sarajevo?'

'I'll tell you all about that later.'

'No. Now.'

'All right. Things are getting better over there. There's talk of a peace agreement. Carla's fine. She's back in Rome with her husband. Everyone's fine.'

'And Željko?'

'He's disappeared.'

'Disappeared?'

'Yes. After your report and the piece Carla did about him, everybody wanted to interview him, but he just disappeared, like a puff of smoke.'

'Perhaps he's talking to his ghosts,' she whispers.

'Perhaps.'

* * *

Much later Colin says, 'I must go.'

'Why? Stay.' She doesn't want to be alone.

'I can't.' He looks awkward.

'What is it? There's something you're not telling me.' She can see how uncomfortable he is.

'No. It's not my business. Let your mother ...'

'My mother?'

'... or the doctor tell you.'

'Tell me what?' she says, suddenly frightened. 'That I'm going to die?'

'No,' he says, 'it's not that, thank God.'

'Well then, what?'

'Your mother told me. We've become good friends while you've been lying here, unconscious.' It's obvious that he doesn't want to say any more.

'Told you what?' She's trying to sit up, but the pain is stopping her. 'Told you what?' She's nearly shouting now.

'Do you really want me to say it?'

'Yes. Yes.' She knows something big is coming, something that will change her life forever. She doesn't know if she's ready for it. She doesn't know if she's strong enough.

Colin stands up and goes over to the window. He stands with his back to her, scratching his head. Then he turns round, his face twisted in a half-smile.

'You're pregnant, Katy.'

'I'm pregnant?' She almost laughs. Is he trying to be funny?

'It's not a joke. You're pregnant, Katy. Twins.'

111

'Twins? Twins?' she asks, confused.

'Yes. There's no doubt. Two of them!'

She lies back down on the bed, staring at the ceiling. Twins. Two children. Two little girls perhaps, running into the afternoon. She can see them already, getting up from the dusty ground by the railway, carrying their plastic can, running past the railway line, into the garden, dancing in the sunlight. For a second she can almost hear the sound of laughter. Twins.

Colin is standing by the bed. His face has gone red; his blue eyes look uncertain. He clears his throat.

'Look … umm, Katy, if you want me to go … I mean it must be a shock.'

'Don't go.' In her heart there is music.

She looks at his face. She has never really noticed the kindness in it before. 'Stay with me, Colin. For today, at least. Stay with me.'

He takes her hand as he stands there by the bed, and for a long time there's no sound in the room except for the ticking of the hospital clock, as the light goes from the day.

Katy's mind is racing. Twins, she thinks. Twins. Željko, dear Željko. Colin next to her, so strong, so safe. 'It's going to be all right,' she tells herself. 'It's going to be all right.'

And as she falls gradually back into sleep, she hears it again – the solo saxophone, a cry in the dark, its beautiful melody piercing her heart, telling her, singing to the people of Sarajevo, singing to the whole world that even now in the middle of all our suffering, even now as the shells rain down and the guns spit and kill, telling us that love goes on and on.